REMEMBERING
THE
FUTURE

REMEMBERING THE FUTURE

The Challenge of the Churches in Europe

Robert C. Lodwick

Editor

Friendship Press • New York

We are grateful to several publishers and authors for permission to reprint excerpts from their publications. These sources are cited where the excerpts appear.

Scripture quotations are from the New Revised Standard Version of the Bible, copyright © 1989 by the Division of Christian Education of the National Council of the Churches of Christ in the USA. Used by permission. All rights reserved.

Editorial Offices:
475 Riverside Drive, New York, NY 10015

Distribution Offices:
P.O. Box 37844, Cincinnati, OH 45222-0844

Manufactured in the United States of America

99 98 97 96 95   5 4 3 2 1

Layout and design by Carol Gorgun

Library of Congress Cataloging–in–Publication Data

Remembering the future: the challenge of the churches in Europe/Robert C. Lodwick, editor.
    p.   cm.
    ISBN 0-377-00290-9
    1. Christianity—Europe. 2. Europe—Religion. 3. Ecumenical movement. 4. Church and social problems—Europe. 5. Church and state—Europe. I. Lodwick, Robert C.
    BR735.R455 1995
    274'.0829—dc20
                                         94-39489
                                             CIP

Contents

Central Europe

Eastern Europe

The Balkans

Conclusion

Map by Ruth Soffer

Acknowledgments

Becoming the editor of a Friendship Press book in mid-stream is a daunting process. Writers had been selected, some manuscripts were in hand while others were missing, deadlines were drawing closer. All in all, it was made easier by the earlier preparations of Mark Stokoe, who had worked with the Program Committee on Education for Mission on the outline for the book and had selected many of the writers. Tom Dorris, a longtime friend and colleague, submitted his final manuscript just days before his untimely death in an automobile accident in Sweden. I have had the privilege of knowing personally many of the authors who have contributed to this book and who have shared with us their faith, their understandings, and their remembering of the future.

A special word of thanks must go to Paul Mojzes who gave unstintingly of his time in bringing clarity to the complex issues in the former Yugoslavia. Likewise Barbara Green undertook a special task in adding a brief but comprehensive "Afterword" to the manuscript of Bishop Krusche. Those who read the manuscripts prior to going to press are always an important help to the editor.

I must add that it was a joy to work with the staff of Friendship Press, who became my guides, critics, advisors, and friends. I feel I know them well through many conversations by phone, fax, e-mail, and FedEx. Thank you for the learnings that I have had in this process of preparing this book.

And finally, without the help of my wife, Hedwig, I would have never met the deadlines. Hedy proofread, corrected, wrote, and wondered aloud about our so-called retirement during these hectic weeks. But we both love Europe, learned much during our years there and continue to be enriched in the process of "remembering the future" with its challenges for the churches in Europe.

—Robert C. Lodwick

Preface

Jean Fischer

As general secretary of the Conference of European Churches, known affectionately as CEC, I am grateful that the Friendship Press 1995-96 study themes for the churches in North America will be Europe as well as the United Nations. As we all know, both are playing a crucial role in today's world. The CEC has had close ties with the National Council of the Churches of Christ in the USA and the Canadian Council of Churches during the years of the Cold War and since then, as so many new developments have affected both of our continents.

Our work together in the Churches Human Rights Program, which has accompanied the Conference on Security and Cooperation in Europe, has been greatly appreciated and, hopefully, will continue as the CSCE moves into a new phase of its activity. On behalf of our three councils, Joan B. Campbell, general secretary of the NCCC-USA, Alexandra F. Johnston, president of the Canadian Council of Churches, and I have just sent a letter to the foreign ministers and secretary of state, of the governments of the signatory states of the Helsinki Final Act regarding the Budapest Review Conference of the CSCE now in progress. Our letter raised three major concerns of the churches: national minorities, religious freedom and church-state relations, and racism and xenophobia.

I welcome your study and hope the readers will be able to see Europe whole without the divisions that were so prevalent in the past. It is appropriate that the title of this book uses part of the theme of the recent assembly of the Ecumenical Forum of European Christian Women, "Remembering the Future." The divisions of the past should remind us of what we need to avoid in the future as we seek to work together in church and society.

The rush to freedom during the past five years has created new problems and challenges for the churches in Eastern Europe. At the same time, the rush to the East by missionaries from the West has threatened the ecumenical spirit that had been built through painstaking efforts during the years of oppression and repression. It is our hope, however, that working together, the 118 member churches of CEC from all countries of Europe can contribute to reconciliation and a more just society. In 1997, the Conference of European Churches with the Council of European Bishops' Conferences of the Roman Catholic Church is planning an all European assembly, the theme of which will be "Reconciliation: God's Gift and Source of New Life."

We seek your prayers and pray that God will bless you in your study and in your witness to Jesus Christ.

—Jean Fischer,
General Secretary of the Conference of European Churches
October 15, 1994

Introduction

Robert C. Lodwick and Mark Stokoe

"Be Not Afraid: Remember the Future!" This was the theme of the 1994 General Assembly of the Ecumenical Forum of European Christian Women. "Remember the future!" Is this not a contradiction in

terms? Ordinarily we remember the past and plan for the future. The more we thought about these words, however, the more appropriate they seemed for the churches in today's complex, troubled, exciting, and changing Europe.

Remember the future! For Christians, to live in the future is a sign of faith and hope that overcomes doubt and despair. Peace communities in Northern Ireland have had the courage to work for years in a nation torn by killings and retaliatory killings by remembering the future. Women in Black and other peace organizations have been demonstrating against the horrors of war in the former Yugoslavia because they want to remember the future.

While headlines in the newspapers and on the evening news have reported the tragedies of Rwanda, Haiti, Somalia and Bosnia, they have also shown a glimpse of the future for a peaceful Northern Ireland, and a possible new future of peaceful coexistence for Palestinians and Israelis. Thousands of Russian Orthodox *babushkas*, the

grandmothers who remained believers during the past seventy years, remembered the future as they, in their own way, took responsibility for the education in the faith of their grandchildren.

A very new old world

In the past seven years, to use a biblical measure of time, changes on a biblical scale have occurred throughout Europe. Mighty empires have collapsed and ancient animosities have resurfaced. A respected colleague has suggested that the resurrection of these animosities is a result of a selfish quest for power by some political leaders, providing a basis for hatred and violence against their contemporary neighbors. In any case, these power struggles have ignited terrible wars, causing whole peoples to be forced into exile. At the same time, European culture is flowering as never before. The ancient cities of Prague, Warsaw, and Budapest have reemerged as vibrant centers of world class theater, art, and music. Even in the new and unfamiliar European

Mennonite mother and sons in Brussels

Art Smoker

capitals of Bratislava, Skopje, and Zagreb, cultures long-suppressed or simply overlooked are being reborn.

Actively engaged in these changes are the Christians of Europe and their churches. To their credit, it was Christians, and young people working through their churches, who played key roles in bringing down the oppressive communist regimes in eastern and central Europe. Many Christians in these lands are now taking the lead in rebuilding their shattered societies. Like the East, western Europe, too, is challenged to build new forms of political, economic, and social life. Here, too, Christians, churches, and church-related institutions are playing a cautionary, yet creative and sometimes prophetic role, particularly in relation to issues of social justice, in the creation of the ever-expanding European Union.

Unfortunately, the churches and Christians of Europe are directly involved in the troubles of the Old World as well. Fueled by differing cultures and politics, Eastern Orthodox Christians, Roman Catholics, and Muslims fight in the former Yugoslavia, and Protestants struggle with Eastern Orthodox for the hearts and minds of Russia. Even as the nations of the Old World reconcile themselves to new unity—or new divisions—so too, the Christian churches of Europe struggle with these new realities.

In Germany, where Protestants of East and West were compelled for political reasons to have separate structures, they are now reunited. In Ukraine, formerly united Orthodox have fallen into schism. In Poland, the Czech Republic, Slovakia, and Hungary, the Roman Catholic Church, at one time dominant, at another time oppressed, seeks a new way of relating to these states, and has reasserted itself in church-state affairs. In every country of Europe, Christians and their churches are tested by secularism, streams of refugees, pollution, the painful changes required by cultural pluralism, political turmoil, economic dislocation, and theological change. It is an exciting, challenging, sometimes dangerous, but always fascinating time to be a Christian in Europe.

The churches and Christians of Europe

This book seeks to tell of the churches of Europe today. It tells of the Christian men and women who belong to them, who serve them, who witness to the gospel of Christ through them. It is neither comprehensive nor complete, for the story of the churches of Europe is first the story of the Old World, of Christian communities that have been worshipping, praying, and serving Christ for almost two thousand years. That story and its current chapters would require volumes, rather than a simple book.

This book, however, is intended as an introduction for North Americans to the new Europe, its churches and the role of the churches in the creation of the new Europe. Parts will seem familiar for many Christians in North America, whether Protestant, Catholic, or Eastern Orthodox, who are descendants of European immigrants who once belonged to these European churches. Many of the churches of Europe are truly "mother" churches from which have sprung many of the denominations in North America. To study Europe is, in part, to study ourselves, for we share a common past. However, we are aware that this is not true for Native Americans and many African and Asian sisters and brothers who are members of these churches and who have brought their own rich gifts to church life in the Americas.

Terminal fatigue?

While there is a shared past, Christianity in Europe and North America can be very different in worship, theological emphases, customs, and traditions. The roles of women and the issues of racism, nationalism, human rights, and religious freedom are all approached from different perspectives. To study these differences can be enlightening and challenging. More importantly, to study Europe and its churches is to share in the future of the Christian mission as a whole.

On the other hand, there are those who argue that the Old World and its churches suffer from terminal fatigue. Europe is no longer "Christendom." It is increasingly secular, increasingly capitalist, and increasingly materialistic. Can the ancient churches of Europe renew themselves? Fifteen years ago, the Friendship Press mission study was also on Europe and the title of the study book was *Must Walls Divide?* by James E. Will. Now we have seen the old walls disappear but have watched as new walls are taking their places. The preface to Will's book stated that it is worthwhile "to stress the fact that, although there are considerable differences in practical circumstances, it can be argued validly that the churches in all parts of Europe are facing the same basic challenge. North, south, east and west, the secularization of modern peoples is either actively corroding the church or simply ignoring its existence." These words still ring true today.

Throughout this book, almost every author has referred to secularism, the pervasive nature of secularism, the dominant influence of secular structures in today's society, or the threat of secularism within and to the life of the church. There was a period in history when religion or the church dominated the culture of Europe, whether the world of Byzantium, or the Roman Empire, or the Orthodox Church, or the Catholic Church, or the world of the Reformation. In today's Europe, however, religious forces must contend with the growing appeal of secularism. According to *Webster's New World Dictionary*, secularism is "the belief that religion and ecclesiastical affairs should not enter into the functions of the state." Wherever governments or segments of society have become secular, they disregard, think inappropriate, or reject practices of religious faith and worship related to state or civic life. The concern over the growing secular nature of society is a major issue for churches in Europe and North America as they rethink the form of their witness and mission in society.

Christians in Europe: A brief overview

Europe, which extends from small islands in the Atlantic Ocean, across great plains to the Ural mountains far in the east, is, in fact, the second smallest of the world's seven continents. It is, however, the second most populous, with over 600 million inhabitants, more than twice the number of people in Canada and the United States combined. Europe is divided into 53 nations, in which 189 different languages are spoken and six different alphabets are used.

Christianity has been in Europe since biblical times. We do not usually think of Europe when we think of the Bible, but if we are to understand the Christians of Europe, we must. The Bible tells us that a European government (the Roman Empire) condemned Christ; its soldiers tormented him, crucified him and later stood guard at his tomb. The Bible also tells us that it was a European who first bore public witness to Christ's divinity at the cross: "Now when the centurion, who stood facing him, saw that in this way he breathed his last, he said, 'Truly this man was God's Son!'" (Mark 15:39) Six of the books of the New Testament are addressed to churches in Europe.

As the Bible bears witness, European Christianity was the fruit of the earliest Christian missionaries. "During the night Paul had a vision: there stood a

Skateboarder draws crowd beside Notre Dame Cathedral in Paris

man of Macedonia pleading with him and saying, 'Come over to Macedonia and help us.' When he had seen the vision, we immediately tried to cross over to Macedonia, being convinced that God had called us to proclaim the good news to them." (Acts 16:9-11) Twenty centuries later, the overwhelming majority of Europeans is, at least nominally, Christian. Most are members of one of three great families of Christian churches, the Roman Catholic, Eastern Orthodox, and Protestant churches.

The Roman Catholic Church

A majority of Christians in Europe (some 350 million) are members of the Catholic Church, the spiritual and administrative center of which has been in Rome since the first century. Catholicism, it has been argued, created Europe. The reverse might also be said to be true. Even today, more than half of all Catholic priests in the world are Europeans. Alone among Christian churches, and indeed among the religions of the world, Roman Catholicism possesses its own sovereign state, Vatican City. Half the size of New York City's Central Park, the Vatican is on a hill overlooking ancient Rome. It is the last remnant of the Roman Catholic Church's once great secular power. Joseph Stalin, the ruthless Soviet dictator, once dismissed both the Roman Catholic Church and its tiny European state with the famous question: "And how many divisions does the Pope have?" But the fact is, after fifty years Stalin and his great European empire are gone, while the Roman Catholic Church and its tiny European city-state, ruled by the present pope, John Paul II, continues to exert influence throughout the world, as seen by its recent controversial role in the United Nations Conference on Population held in Cairo in 1994.

Since the reforms of the Second Vatican Council (1961-63), the Roman Catholic Church in Europe, as in North America, has undergone profound changes. Like their North American co-religionists, European Catholics celebrate the Mass in their local languages, rather than in Latin as had been traditional for centuries. European Catholicism is different from Catholicism in the U.S. and Canada, however, in that it still retains a strong folk, or ethnic, element. Even in the most secularized countries, saints' days and other religious holidays can be celebrated by all, Catholic and non-Catholic alike, in colorful and festive style. Monasticism, too, plays a greater role in European Catholic spirituality than among Catholics in North America, if only because of the far greater number of convents and monasteries in Europe. Veneration of the Virgin Mary, spurred on by recent reported appearances of the Virgin in such diverse places as Medjugorje, Bosnia; El Escorial, Spain; and Goricheva, Ukraine, is also widespread among Catholics in Europe.

Perhaps the greatest difference between European and American Catholicism, however, is the reemergence of Catholic nationalism in Europe. For many, to be authentically Polish, for example, requires one to be Roman Catholic. This fusion of national identity and religious faith among Catholics is no less motivating in Ireland, at the edge of western Europe, as it is in Slovakia in central Europe, or in Croatia in the Balkans. Pope John Paul II's vision of a re-Christianized Europe following the collapse of communism is less of an ecumenical vision than it is the vision of Catholic Europe as known and experienced in his native Poland.

The Eastern Orthodox and Protestants

The second greatest number of Christians in Europe belong to the family of Eastern Orthodox Churches, whose 160 million members are located mainly in Russia, the Balkans, and eastern Europe. Like the Catholic Church, the spiritual head of the Eastern Orthodox Church also resides in Europe, in the ancient city of Constantinople (now known as Istanbul) in that small part of Turkey that lies in Europe. Protestants, together with the Anglicans (the Church of England), form the third great family of Christians in Europe, with more than 130 million members. They are the majority denomination and/or official state churches in many European countries, especially in northern Europe.

The differences between these three families of Christian churches are theological, cultural, and social. For one thousand years, until 1054, the Eastern Orthodox and Roman Catholic Churches were united as one. Thus, they share many similarities in administration, spirituality, and doctrine. Over the centuries of division, however, the two churches have grown steadily apart. While continuing to recognize a three-fold ministry of bishops, priests, and deacons, Orthodox do not accept the universal jurisdiction or the infallibility of the pope of Rome. Eastern Orthodoxy remains as it was in its earliest days, a mystical, ascetical faith that prizes its unchanging adherence to early Christian traditions. As a result, worship in the Orthodox Church, unlike the contemporary Roman Catholic or Protestant churches, remains highly ritualistic and formalized. Monasticism among the Orthodox plays a more profound role even than among Roman Catholics. It is to monasteries, male or female, that Orthodox Christians often take their infants to be baptized; to monasteries that Orthodox widows and widowers retire upon the death of their spouses; and from monasteries where new bishops are selected.

Among the Protestant churches of Europe there exists the same diversity in theologies, worship styles, and ministries that one would find in Protestant churches in North America. There are scores of Protestant churches in Europe, although the greatest number of Europeans, by far, belong to but four denominational families: Lutheran (70 million), Reformed (30 million), Baptist (8 million), and Methodist (5 million). Some non-Catholic, non-Orthodox Christian churches that predate the 16th century Protestant Reformation, such as the followers of Jan Hus in the Czech Republic, or the Waldensian Church of Italy, are an integral part of the Protestant family of churches, as is the Church of England (Anglican), which claims 25 million members. There is a rapidly growing number of evangelical, charismatic, and Pentecostal churches in most European countries that is increasing in importance in its interaction, or lack of it, with ancient or traditional churches and parish life.

Europe in six parts

Given the size and diversity of Europe and the long history of its Christian communities, this study has divided Europe and its churches into six regions based largely on geography. Only a few years ago a more simple division could have been used: East and West. But today as political boundaries change, new nations emerge, economic systems readjust and populations shift, only physical boundaries—mountains, rivers, and seas—remain constant, but not necessarily as the political boundaries they once were.

Each of the sections in this study is self-contained. Thus, this book may be studied as a whole, through combinations of regions, or with a focus on a single region alone. The large number of authors represented here reflects the diversity of Christianity in Europe. Taken together, these articles form a contemporary mosaic of Christian life in Europe: at times intriguing, at times bewildering, at times inspiring. Readers may differ with the conclusions of certain authors, but we have attempted a broad, representative overview of current realities.

The regions of Europe

Moving from West to East, our European regions begin with the British Isles, an area that includes England, Northern Ireland, Scotland, Wales, and the Republic of Ireland. Sharing a common language and a common culture with much of North America, the churches of the British Isles will seem familiar indeed to a majority of readers, Protestant and Catholic alike.

To the south of the British Isles lies Latin Europe: France, Belgium, Luxembourg, Italy, Malta, Spain, Portugal, and certain regions of Switzerland. Once united by the Roman Empire (from whence its cognate languages are derived), these lands are traditionally Roman Catholic in faith and custom, with the exception of the Protestant French-speaking cantons of Switzerland. Protestant churches exist in all Latin countries. The traditional hostility between Catholics and Protestants has slowly given way to a growing ecumenical cooperation, common concern about the spiritual challenge of a secular society, and to a new interfaith dialogue with the growing number of Muslim immigrants throughout the region. Indeed, Muslims, rather than Protestant Christians, now form the second largest religious group in France.

To the far north lies Scandinavia (Denmark, Norway, Sweden, Finland, Iceland, and the Faroe Islands) as well as the newly emerging Baltic states of Lithuania, Latvia, and Estonia. Lutheranism is the dominant Christian denomination in Latvia and Estonia, but an Eastern Orthodox minority plays a major role in Finland, Estonia, and Latvia. Lithuania, with its close cultural and ancient political and religious ties with Poland, remains steadfastly Catholic. Northern Christianity is unique in Europe in many ways, for nowhere in Europe is the culture so secularized and, paradoxically, the Protestant state churches so established, as in the countries of the North.

In central Europe, Germany, the Netherlands, and northern Switzerland have been mainly Protestant since the Reformation of the sixteenth century. Here Lutheranism and the Reformed Churches predominate. Today, as Germany struggles with reunification, the Protestant churches play a key role in promoting civil unity, ecological balance, and social justice for refugees and immigrants. Austria has always played an important role in central European political affairs. Passed over in the East-West simplicities of the Cold War, the largely Catholic nations of Poland, Hungary, the Czech Republic, and Slovakia are historically part of central Europe and are among the most dynamic cultural centers today. However, rapid economic growth in some and economic decline in others contributes to a general political instability throughout the region. Here a reinvigorated Roman Catholic Church is once again dominant, fueling Protestant and Orthodox fears that the power of the majority in the new democracies might threaten religious freedom, just as did forty years of Communist rule. Since receiving independence, Croatia and Slovenia are considered by some to be

Sunday lunch in London Mennonite Center garden

5

part of central Europe, but in this study and on the map they are listed as part of the Balkans, where they had been states of the former Yugoslavia. Two articles in this section deal extensively with the life of the church during the Communist era. The reader will find these longer articles exceedingly important in understanding both the role of the church and the oppression by the state during the years of the Communist regime.

Eastern Europe, our fifth region, truly refers again to nations not in the center, but in the eastern third of Europe. Together with Russia, these new nations of Ukraine, Moldova, Belarus, Georgia, Azerbaijan, and Armenia are still reeling from the collapse of the Soviet Union. Loosely united in its successor union, the Commonwealth of Independent States (CIS), these nations struggle merely to survive. Civil war torments some and threatens them all. The churches, most of all the Russian Orthodox Church, having suffered more than seventy years of brutal oppression, struggle too, attempting to bring hope amid deep despair and societal decay. Their stories are perhaps among the most inspiring of all the stories of Christian Europe.

Finally, to the South, lies the Balkans. A byword in the Anglo-Saxon world for troubled politics, where the ethnic, religious, and cultural jumble resulting from millennia of warfare, conquest, and invasion continues. Although freed from the communists, Albania, Macedonia, and Romania have greater difficulty emerging from the social chaos that resulted from those years of communist rule. Meanwhile, some of the states of the former Yugoslavia—Serbia, Montenegro, and Bosnia-Herzegovina—have sunk further into darkness through a terrible and vicious war whereas Slovenia has avoided being drawn into that war and has prospered in its newly recognized nationhood. Croatia, on the other hand, is still caught up in the conflict with Serbia and Bosnia-Herzegovina. Three articles on the Balkans, including one of a theological nature, seek to help us understand that complex and volatile area.

The southernmost corner of the Balkans, and hence of Europe, has its own set of problems. Greece threatens its neighbor Macedonia in a dispute over a name and an ancient symbol on a flag, while Turkey warily watches for mistreatment of Muslims in Bosnia, Bulgaria, and Greece. Alas, the lovely island of Cyprus, which will not be included in this study, remains divided still, fully twenty years after the invasion and partition of the largely Greek island by Turkey. In the Balkans, Christians, mainly Eastern Orthodox, do not understand their faith as a Sunday morning phenomenon or a personal choice. Here faith defines a person's ethnicity, nationality, language and, hopefully, where she or he may live in safety. However, as Marlin VanEldren, former editor of *One World,* the monthly magazine of the World Council of Churches, has written, "As one looks at the Balkans, it is clear from many claims and counter-claims, that the seeds are being sown for a violently divergent harvest of future historical memories."

A final word

Europe is very much a part of the world scene and therefore needs also to be understod from the perspective of other peoples. Recently the prime minister of Malaysia said that most of Europe still had to get rid of an attitude of incredible arrogance. "The age of hegemony has not yet quite passed. It should die away. We should bury it." We invited John Pobee of Ghana to share his view of Europe as an African. We all need to listen to each other. Therefore, this book is intended as the first word, rather than the last, on the lives and peoples of the churches of Europe today. Given by faithful Christians in the Old World, it is a word that we need to hear and reflect upon so that together, in examining the past, we can remember the future.

Remembering THE FUTURE

British Isles

John Nurser

The Churches in Britain

In this century, the United States and Great Britain have had a special relationship forged through history and two world wars. Through these wars, when we nearly experienced defeat, we in Britain were helped first by countries of the Empire, and later by the United States.

When the Americans entered these wars, we believed, rightly, that victory was as good as settled. This talk, on both sides of the Atlantic, of a "special relationship" has been a rather comforting idea, a family Christmas-dinner kind of toast, but, in practical politics, an illusion.

In the summer of 1994, President Bill Clinton made a speech in Berlin in which this illusion became painfully apparent. He was very gentle when he said that Americans will always think of Britain and the British people with affection. He also noted the obvious in that we share a common language. And we share the law and literature and Christian culture that the founding fathers brought across the Atlantic. But, he told his audience in Berlin, the center of gravity of Washington's policy in the European theater is now Germany, the keystone of the European Union. Those of us who read or heard his speech realized that the "special relation-

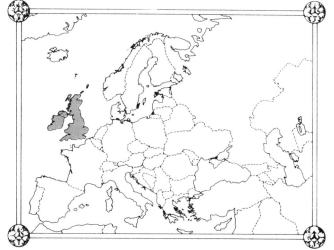

ship" with us, like so many partnerships in modern family life, was no longer at center stage.

The United States is a very unusual country among the main protagonists of World War II in that it has not lost an empire, in the traditional sense of blocks of color on the map. Russia, France, Italy, Britain, Japan, the Netherlands, Belgium, Portugal—they are all now smaller, a lot smaller, with less clout. The USA is just about the same size as it was then.

In Britain's case, the dynamic that led to reduction was as much from within Britain as from the present-day independent states of the former Empire (most of them now still members of the multiracial and multinational British Commonwealth). So it was a peaceful change. But it led to two important shifts. First, there was a shift of population in the 1950s and 1960s; large-scale immigration to the big cities of Britain from the West Indies and South Asia was welcomed. Second, after the end of Empire around 1960 the higher echelons of British industry and government came to the conclusion that Britain could no longer go it alone.

Psychologically, there seemed to be a choice between closer integration with America or with the newly flourishing European Economic Community, based in Brussels. Ordinary people were happy enough staying as we were in the days of the Pilgrim Fathers, a middle-sized island off the northwestern coast of Europe, independent of anybody.

Unfortunately, there was never any real public debate in Britain, and the consequences of that omission are coming home to roost. The great post-World War II European project has now, with the Maastricht Treaty, come to the end of what can be done in cosmopolitan tower blocks by legal and economic engineers and, for the first time, depends on the skill of politicians in winning consent. (The Treaty on European Union was signed in February 1992 in Maastricht, Netherlands, by representatives of the twelve member nations of the European Community. The treaty called for establishing a common currency for all member countries as well as common foreign and security policies. While ratified, its full implementation has been delayed by internal politics of member nations.)

This is the point at which the religious landscape makes a difference to politicians. It is a real test of skill to win consent for a major shift of national policy, especially when it involves how we see neighbors. All that politicians ever have to work with are our national stories, our familiar grammar of persuasion and our deepest shared sense of what human life means.

Sir Edward Heath, the British Prime Minister who took us into Europe in 1973, is someone who sees the whole logic of "Europe" in the 20th century as requiring British membership. His bitter enemy and successor as leader of the Conservative Party, Margaret Thatcher, has always been a reluctant European, far more deeply attracted by the vision with which Ronald Reagan's rhetoric captivated the American electorate. During the 1980s, in the very years when Prime Minister Thatcher signed the Single European Act, Britain was more American in ethos than it has ever been. They were the years of the individual as consumer, the aggressive boss, short-term profits (not too many enquiries about how they were made), destruction of participatory government, and a general ridicule of "common good" or "society" or "failure."

Her disciples within the present government are vehemently opposed to what they call European federalism (in their special usage, meaning centralization). The title of "European Union" is anathema. British officials in the "Brussels bureaucracy" are accused of "going native." This causes paralyzing internal stresses in Parliament; especially when there is a very small majority. Businessmen know that to begin to unravel British membership of what (since 1993) is the European Union would bring economic catastrophe. To be stereotyped as persistently and ungraciously dragging our feet is not the best way to promote the City of London's role as financial hub of Europe.

A decade of self-doubt

There is a powerful movement in Britain called Charter 88, which is dedicated to the proposition that our institutions are so unexamined and behind the times that they are a handicap and a disgrace. For example, we do not have a constitution; our human rights are so badly protected that British cases clog the Council of Europe's Court of Human Rights at Strasbourg.

> There is a powerful movement in Britain called Charter 88, which is dedicated to the proposition that our institutions are so unexamined and behind the times that they are a handicap and a disgrace.

The last five years have seen dramatic undermining of public confidence in the most symbolic of British institutions: High Court judges, cabinet ministers, universities, the banks, Lloyds the insurers, our national football teams. Too few young people play cricket. Even the monarchy itself, the keystone of establishment, has suffered. It may not be possible in our media world ever to recover its lost aura of mystery.

The theater of deference, so characteristic of modern British (or at least English) society, has had to put up its shutters. The (Anglican) Church of England "by law established" is no longer plausible as the religion of the English people, who wherever they live, still have rights in their parish church. The same could be said of the (Presbyterian) Church of

Ordination of women at Canterbury Cathedral

A Historic Moment

In March 1994, after years of heated debate and controversy, the Church of England ordained its first women priests. Since then, over six hundred women have been ordained. After the first group of women was ordained, the archbishop of Canterbury, George Carey, demonstrated his own support for women priests by ordaining twenty-two to the priesthood in May.

The Ecumenical Press Service reported the archbishop as describing the ordination as a "historic moment" and in his view a good moment. Carey said it was nevertheless tinged with sadness. "None of us wants this service to be the cause of dissension and division in the body of Christ, but for some it is. No woman I know seeking ordination desires to be a focus of disunity; yet, against her will, she finds she is." Addressing the women, Carey said, "We should not jump to the conclusion that your ordination is in some sense incomplete. It is not. But not everyone has received it. The whole church, including yourselves, has to live with the sadness of this, and the inward hurt that not everyone, even in your own church, is able to accept you in their hearts and minds as a 'real' priest on a par with men, although your legal and canonical status will be beyond dispute."

As the result of the ordination of women, some two hundred Anglican priests have either resigned their ministry or indicated their firm intention of doing so because they cannot in conscience continue to serve in a church that ordains women priests. Of these, between 75 and 100 have been received into communion with Rome over the past two years and another 75 or 100 are expected to do so during 1995.

Of the thirty-four provinces and member churches of the Anglican Communion worldwide, fifteen have ordained women as deacons, fourteen have ordained women to the priesthood. In addition, there are two bishops who are women. The issue of women's ordination is on the agenda in five other synods: Australia, Southern Africa, Central Africa, the West Indies, and Scotland.

Scotland.

In 17th century England, the discipline and unity in religious belief symbolized by bishops was claimed to be a pre-condition of kingship in political life. Perhaps, granted the wall of separation between church and state, the special sense of civil religion in Americanism is a precondition of presidential democracy in the U.S. In other words, politics and culture are dependent upon some sufficient consensus about the deepest values and meanings in life—which may of course, as in the Soviet system, be atheist.

When the American Constitution first astonished the world (it can never last, everyone said), what distinguished it from the Old World of Europe was precisely its leaving church membership to individual choice. It is important to recognize that many Europeans actually preferred, and still prefer, a less conscious but longer-term and more communal sense of belonging. Greece and the Republic of Ireland are still trying (with difficulty) to disentangle church and nation in their modern constitutions. Bosnia is a hellish example of what can happen when religious "nations" live intermingled. In Europe, unlike America, it is rare to transfer from one religious flag to another.

Church-going today

Grace Davie, a sociologist of religion at Exeter University, has described the religion of present-day Europe as believing in belonging rather than doing. A great majority in Britain claims to belong to a particular Christian church. Most still claim to be "C of E" (Church of England). Most claim to believe in God. But as for going to church, that is anoth-

9

Excluded in Silence, Deaf Christians Claim

Ted Harrison

Deaf Christians are often "outside" the church struggling to get in, a deaf woman priest told a conference held for and by deaf lay people and church ministers in Canterbury, England, in September 1994. The conference, called "The Place of Deaf People in the Worldwide Church," was held as issues connected to deafness have caused sharp debate in some Christian and secular circles.

Vera Hunt, the first deaf woman to be ordained in the Anglican church, asked the conference: "Where is the place of deaf people in the church today? We still seem to be outside the doors heaving away to get them fully open."

As awareness of the needs of deaf Christians grows, the British Bible Society has recently released on video the first translation of scripture into British sign language. A new dictionary, called *Lifting Holy Hands*, has also been published by the Church of England, suggesting signs to be used by deaf people in the course of worship.

But all those working in this field face major problems in translating the spoken word into sign language, for some of the signing symbols which have evolved are now deemed to be highly offensive. Britain's sign language users engaged in a heated debate recently after the main television channels decided to ban certain symbols. The symbol for Chinese, which is pulling the eyes to make them look slanted, and the sign for Jew, which suggests a hooked nose, have been ruled inadmissible.

In worship, the special signs published in the new dictionary enable theological ideas, usually formed and developed by the spoken and written word, to be faithfully conveyed. These symbols are designed to enable deaf people both to worship together in separate congregations and to take part in the general life of the church.

Up to 100,000 people in Britain communicate in sign language.

—Ecumenical News International, 94-0037

er matter. Exceptionally in the whole of western Europe, Ireland (Catholic and Protestant) remains a country where it is normal to go to church. Total weekly church attendance in England is about ten percent of the population, split almost equally between Catholics, Anglicans, and Protestants.

Ignorance of the most basic information, such as the Lord's Prayer or the story of Jesus' life, is widespread. There was a point, about 1960, when religious culture was no longer passed on as part of the general culture. Religion is no longer allowed serious public status. So the old-style establishment, with Anglican bishops sitting by right in Parliament, has lost its roots. This has debilitating consequences, and is to be regretted. But it's not easy to see how Humpty can be put together again. Just giving a place to mullahs and cardinals and televangelists and rabbis in the House of Lords would not do the trick.

There was a watershed between the Egyptian nationalization of the Suez Canal (1956) and the student revolts of 1968. Being British could suddenly mean to be of Afro-Caribbean or South Asian heritage. Islam became bigger than Methodism. Youth culture was invented, which not only gave acceptability to drugs, but—intentionally or not—developed a kind of music that excluded the parent generation and pulverized it with boom boxes. They were also the years when a secure two-parent family became no longer the norm. Teenagers and young adults rarely come through now after having even a nominal commitment to church. The men and women under 45 years old in British churches are not only a relatively small cohort. They have, much more than in the past, either been "converted" or have "camped" in the church buildings.

Let me explain. The active religious groups in high school are likely to be evangelical, with a sense of having chosen to opt out of what "everybody does" in the wider society. The lively and well-attended churches are strong on personal relationships with God and within the group, on the authority of the Bible, and on a sharp definition of boundaries, whether in belief or behavior. The informal nondenominational house church makes a potent claim to be the model of New Testament Christianity. There is a playing down of the local secular community and its medieval parish church.

When I speak of "camping" on church territory, I am thinking of two groups. Neither of these may feel any particular need to be convinced by the traditional Christian creeds, or to read the Bible, or to give any supernatural authority to clergy. They see the church as a user-friendly arena, the spiritual heritage that we have been given. They take meditation, whether weekly yoga or Ignatian retreats, seriously. Our tradition happens to be Christian; it is rich and open to spiritual growth and to imaginative and intellectual stimulation. So, Britain has a marvelous record of professional and amateur performance of music—much of which tends to happen in churches. The cathedrals are flourishing as they have not done since before the Reformation and, significantly, they have very few committees or organizations.

Following from the tradition (now struggling) of industrial mission, there is a growing sense that the churches are one of the few platforms in our society from which to mount a critique of what the "principalities and powers of this world" are up to. A prime example is the way in which the peaceful overturning of the communist regime in East Germany depended on the availability of open discussion in church buildings.

Third World development is a moral imperative to which the old missionary societies have made a huge contribution. For a whole generation, British Christians have spoken publicly and prayed for the abolition of apartheid in South Africa. It is almost impossible to imagine how the great web of voluntary associations that make up the quality of public life—Amnesty International, marriage counseling, scouts, Oxfam, environmental groups—could continue without the initiative and day-to-day contribution of Christians, often distanced from church practice.

Christian ministry

With this disparate membership it has become difficult to run churches as organized institutions.

The Christian clergy no longer form a recognized profession. There are now far fewer of them, they are equipped with less knowledge, and are usually entering on a second career. Their working relationships are with a denominational manager figure and his bureaucracy on the one hand, and with subscribing members of the worshipping congregation on the other. There is almost no time for general reading or for a public role in the local community. This is a major change in the perception of the Church of England parson. The present orthodoxy (though reality may never catch up with it) is that the stipendiary clergy—employed and paid by the denomination—are there to enable the ministry of the congregation. The individual clergyperson will normally be the focus of a team of trained lay (and ordained) non-stipendiary pastors of both sexes drawn from the congregation. As the structures of all the churches have become more democratic yet more bureaucratic, the authority of the minister or priest is of a different kind. Koinonia (community fellowship) is the buzz-word of church conferences.

The downside of this shift is that involvement in church takes up far more time. It is also less easy to take personal initiatives (I suspect that this is one reason why the churches, especially the Catholics, are finding it so hard to recruit clergy), and for a lay person active in his or her career to play a role in church affairs at the national or local level.

The charismatic wing of the churches has bred sects. Partly because to talk convincingly about the Holy Spirit requires (often excessive) confidence in personal experience. Cults of personality often develop around

The Most Rev. Olu Abiola Co-President, CCBI

Aladura Church in England: More Time for Prayer

The church I lead is named the Aladura International Church. Aladuraism has become an umbrella word for the Nigerian independent churches. Since the 1930s Aladura has referred to those who live a life of prayer and fasting in order to help others. We are neither Spiritualists nor Pentecostals. We mostly live in London. Our church was formed from a Church of England background in 1968, partly because we felt we did not have enough space for prayer. Our services normally go on for three or four hours; it is left to God when they will end. I suppose that a symptom of what worries me about the new ecumenical instruments, such as the Council of Churches of Britain and Ireland (CCBI), is how hard it was for us to find money to continue the spirituality project of the former British Council of Churches (BCC), before the Catholic church became a member.

There is so little finance in the CCBI at the moment to do what needs to be done. The BCC's "Black and White Church the leaders of such groups, helping to attract media coverage. The bureaucratization and consequent "wrinklification" of traditional church leadership, as well as their perceived lack of conviction as teachers, has given the more nimble-footed charismatic and Bible-based groups an advantage. This trend is also true within the denominations. The great influential networks among young people are based on gatherings, pilgrimages, and various other events in places like Corrymeela, Iona, and, in France, Taizé. (See related article on pages 54–60.)

For the Church of England, these developments make for a period of frighteningly rapid change. A body now composed largely of enthusiasts and bureaucrats, it certainly used not to be. A church that claimed to represent the nation, that had responsibility for well over half the heritage buildings listed of national importance, that inherited great endowments from a thousand years ago (but had not a penny of income from the state), suddenly finds itself having to levy substantial income from its worshipping members. Half the nation claims to be non-worshipping/non-paying members. What happens then? Are they to be left out of account until they ask for a funeral?

In all this, we are not ministering to an age that sees itself as unspiritual. Few local bookshops have a section on religion or Bible now, but they all stock manuals of meditation or astrology. A psychiatrist tells me his patients declare themselves almost equally troubled by sexual and spiritual problems. Literature is full of religion, but not of churches. Gregorian chant from a Spanish monastery was at the top of the pop music charts in 1994. Nearly two-thirds of the general population declares itself to have had a religious experience.

What good things might Britain bring to the new Europe?

Surprisingly, there is still antagonism between Catholic and Protestant, Catholic and Orthodox, Christian and Muslim (not to mention Jew) in mainland Europe. Britain has much more a sense of a spectrum of possibilities, among which it is possible to move fairly easily to find friends and colleagues.

Britain has worked out common religious (rather than church) institutions for engaging with at least some important public tasks. For example, nondenominational theology is a recognized discipline in state universities; similarly, religious studies is a subject in state schools; there are chaplains to hospitals and to industry; there is a church advisory committee for religous programs on radio and television.

The imperial inheritance has given Britain and its churches a particular knowledge about and concern for the other continents. The poor of the two-thirds world are not likely to be forgotten. However inadequate it is, we do at least have a functioning legal apparatus against racial discrimination. Other countries do not.

Finally, as Jacques Delors, the former president of the European Commission (and a practicing Catholic) has so often said, without some common humanly persuasive vision the Europe of Brussels cannot last—ought not to last. The Christian churches can, if they have courage, make the gospel contribution that is still the "pearl without price."

Aladura (continued)

Partnership" project at Birmingham was left without a budget. The ecumenical institutions are still at a formative stage. I am afraid the denominations still do their own thing; the black-led churches do not feel equal yet, more like guests than partners. The churches with direct American finance are setting the pace.

I have just returned from a visit to our church in Italy. Because of my color I had a lot of hassle at passport control. We are apprehensive about this move into the European Union. The race situation in general is getting worse. Government policy on immigration encourages people to identify with neo-fascists in calling black people "worthless scroungers." There's a great deal of racist feeling in the police: I have personal experience of that.

But as Christians we have to be optimistic.

—Fr. Olu Abiola

John Nurser

John Nurser is a canon of Lincoln Cathedral and director of Christianity and the Future of Europe in Cambridge, England.

12

Corrymeela staff rock band 'Cantankerous' at 1994 Summerfest

Growing Up in Northern Ireland

Carmel Heaney

When the troops came on to the streets of Northern Ireland in August 1969 I clearly remember my father saying, "It will all be over by Christmas." That was more than twenty-five years ago.

I was ten years old when the current round of "the troubles" began. I grew up on the outskirts of Belfast within earshot of the Lam beg Drum. This was an enormous drum beaten during the annual July 12th Protestant parade commemorating the Protestant victory in the Battle of the Boyne in 1690. The sound of it marked every Twelfth of July, the day of the marches, symbol of Protestant Ulster. I was raised in a Catholic household and attended a Catholic school on the infamous Falls Road. In fact, it was during my school years that I learned about the fascination of violence. I soon got used to the drama of riots and burning buses, the excitement of bomb scares, the tension of shootings across the hockey field. In contrast to the diversions of the day, night life was curtailed by curfew, confined to safe areas, a city scaffolded by silence and cordoned off with checkpoints. I lived with the abnormal as normal, accepting that order and chaos coexisted, that life in Northern Ireland held such promise and yet was deeply paradoxical.

I was sixteen years old when I first came into conversation with Protestants. This conversation explored religious faith and political views and examined what the Ulster poet John Hewitt calls the "break and bond between us." This experience of real meeting and trust was to influence further my adolescence. My membership in the Corrymeela Community, a Christian community working for reconciliation in Northern Ireland, was a direct outcome of my early tentative conversations. It was in this community that I grew to understand my own faith tradition as well as that of my neighbors. I also learned that in divided

Peace at Last?

Robert C. Lodwick

Can peace be a reality in Northern Ireland? This is both a question and a prayer. In Louisville, Kentucky, an editorial cartoon by Hugh Haynie in *The Courier-Journal* used this little poem with sketches of Catholic and Protestant leprechauns toasting each other after the announcement by the Irish Republican Army of a "complete cessation of military operations."

> *The Wee Folk are a wary lot...*
> *And cautious to a fault.*
> *They toast peace in Northern Ireland,*
> *But with a humongous grain of salt.*

The leprechauns were ready to toast again, a bit less cynically this time, when the leaders of the Protestant paramilitary forces called for a cease-fire from their side. This is a further step to peace, as is the new willingness of the British government to hold talks with all parties involved in the conflict. Yet there is still a long road ahead to achieve peace, economic prosperity, and reconciliation.

During the past twenty-five years of civil unrest, 3,170 deaths in Northern Ireland are directly attributable to the "troubles" and tens of thousands of men, women, and children have been wounded or disabled through the violence. Killings or bombing by the Irish Republican Army always brought prompt retaliatory strikes by Protestant paramilitary groups. During numerous previous attempts at peace, cynics have used the phrase, "a problem to every solution!" In its simplest

13

societies one group's fact is another's fiction—that intellectual debate and attempts to convince others were futile. I saw real change happen and real friendships sustained when people began to identify common experiences, talk openly about what difficulties exist, and risk trusting the other.

My sheltered experience of home and school life was broadened to include men and women from very diverse life experiences. I clearly remember at the age of seventeen holding the hand of a woman whose son had been shot dead as a result of sectarian violence, talking to paramilitary leaders over a cup of coffee, planning worship with people from Sri Lanka, discovering my own fears, anxieties, prejudices, and joys all the while.

After school I studied in Belfast and taught for six years in a Convent School in Armagh City. I taught religious studies and many of the students met pupils from the "other side" during those tense years, years of escalating sectarian conflict, years of political polarization. I marveled at the resilience of the students and the commitment of the staff to keep some stability in the midst of instability. Afterwards, I had the good fortune to work full time for the Corrymeela Community. I learned there that it is often the most violent and fearful who have the most to teach me about peace, and that it was a combination of circumstance and luck that brought me into the neighborhood of reconciliation and not violence.

I left Ireland to see it from a distance, to learn about myself away from certainties of people and place. I spent some time working in Oxford before joining the staff of the Council of Churches for Britain and Ireland, where I am happily employed.

When I first heard the announcement of the IRA cessation of violence I shouted for joy, then to my astonishment, I found myself weeping. This mixture of emotions finds me poised between hope and disbelief. The hope of the future masks the realities of seeking to find new ways to live together. Every day that passes without violence gives space and possibility to build a future in trust together.

Carmel Heaney is the Associate Secretary for Youth at the Council of Churches for Britain and Ireland, headquartered in London.

Carmel Heaney

terms, the Catholic minority in Northern Ireland wants to become part of the Irish Republic. The Protestant majority wants to remain part of the United Kingdom.

In recent discussions, one senses that the average IRA member came to believe that future violence will not be productive. When the current "troubles" began, terrorism was a routine method of policy implementation for many countries and often could be financed by appeals to various other sympathetic countries. With the end of the Cold War, it is much harder to raise money for terrorism. Moreover, as terrorism has given way in other places in the world to negotiations as the preferred means of conflict resolution, a general feeling has developed that the same course should be followed in Northern Ireland. At the same time, moral and financial support from the North American Irish community for the IRA's violent campaign has diminished.

The Rev. Sam Hutchinson is clerk of assembly of the Presbyterian Church in Ireland, the largest Protestant denomination in Northern Ireland. In commenting on the ceasefire, he stated, "Every family in Northern Ireland has been affected by the violence, or knows someone who has been affected. The wounds of civil confrontation will take a long time to heal. Yet as painful as our recent history has been, we must not be in bondage to the past. On the other hand, we cannot forget the past, and particularly we cannot forget those who still suffer or grieve because of what has happened in the past.... We realize the enormity of what remains to be done. It will be extremely difficult, like squaring a circle, to reconcile unionist and nationalist perspectives for the future of Ireland."

The Rev. Doug Baker, long-time worker at the Corrymeela Center of Reconciliation, commended the governments of the United Kingdom and of Ireland for their new commitment to work in partnership. "There is a very strong recognition that this is a cease-fire, not peace," he said. "For there to be a peace, a number of issues must be resolved. But now a different atmosphere has been created in which the issues can be discussed."

In the words of the Presbyterian Church of Ireland, "In these fragile days of new beginnings, we need courage, generosity, forgiveness and hope. Inflammatory speech and provocative conduct should be avoided. Public demonstrations and confrontations at this sensitive juncture could easily lead to serious disorder. . . . As we face the long difficult road to an acceptable settlement, both Unionist and Nationalist communities must address themselves not only to their own interests and concerns, but also those of the others in our divided society. All sections of the community will face changes. They should face them graciously."

Christians everywhere are asked to pray about these issues "in the hope that this historic opportunity to reshape the life of Northern Ireland, and all the relationships within these islands, may not be squandered."

Loyalist area of Belfast in 1988

North Dublin School Project mixes children of all faiths and backgrounds in a private effort to undo the prejudice generated by separate Catholic and Protestant schools

15

Churches Together in Pilgrimage

Great Britain has been a pioneer in the Ecumenical Movement. The modern journey towards Christian unity began in Edinburgh in 1910 when a group of missionary leaders from many different denominations met, and realized that the Christian gospel of reconciliation and love in Jesus Christ would not be believed by others while the churches preached it in competition with one another. So in the following thirty years, many enthusiasts for the restoration of Christian unity worked hard to persuade others in their churches to seek unity.

The second stage of the movement for Christian unity in Britain and Ireland began in 1942 in the midst of the Second World War with the formation of the British Council of Churches. The Anglicans and many Protestant churches grouped themselves into a Council so that they could cooperate with one another. They were later joined by the Eastern Orthodox churches. The search for Christian unity became the official policy of these churches and also in the national groupings of churches in Ireland, Scotland, and Wales.

In the first two stages of the movement there had been many attempts to unite different churches at a national level. The only success was that which brought Congregationalists, Presbyterians, and Churches of Christ together in the United Reformed Church. All attempts to bring the Anglicans and free churches closer together in England came to a halt with the failure of Proposals for Covenant in 1982, although a Covenant was established in Wales.

Between 1982 and 1986, many churches continued to pray together and discuss what the next stage of the ecumenical journey should be. Roman Catholics were fully involved in these discussions as were leaders of the so-called "Black-led" churches who had come to Britain from Africa, Asia, and the Caribbean. During Lent 1986 over a million Christians took part in discussion groups on the theme, "What on Earth is the Church For?" They reported back that they wanted the churches to come together in unity, but a unity that found room for the rich diversity already experienced in the different Christian communities.

As a result, the British Council of Churches was transformed into a Council of Churches for Britain and Ireland in September 1990 with new or renewed bodies at national levels in England, Ireland, Scotland and Wales.

A Scottish Experiment in Ecumenism

Maire Gallagher, SND

In 1990, the Scottish Churches' Council was dissolved and replaced by Action of Churches Together in Scotland (ACTS). This change made it possible for the second largest church in Scotland, the Roman Catholic Church, to join but, regretfully, the decision also caused the Baptist Union of Scotland to withdraw its membership. In the short period of the existence of ACTS, immense progress has been made in churches working together. By pooling the resources of the nine member churches and five associate members, ACTS has been enabled to promote common witness in a number of ways.

Within Scotland, ACTS has sought to bring churches together to set up ecumenical teams in the areas of prisons, hospitals, higher education, social ministries, and inner city projects. Some difficulties have arisen over "sacramental ministry" in life-threatening situations and further discussions continue between Protestants and Catholics in this sensitive area.

International efforts include cooperative work in development projects, and in recruiting, preparing, and sending volunteers for overseas mission. A particular concern in mission education has been ACTS's sponsorship of conferences for non-European Christians working for churches in Europe.

At an early stage in its existence, ACTS set up an Interfaith Agency and initiated dialogue with members of the Jewish, Buddhist, Muslim, Hindu, and Sikh communities in Scotland. The support of the churches in funding a post for a field worker in race and interfaith relations was seen as further evidence of their commitment to working with members of different racial and faith communities.

Today, ACTS is recognized throughout Britain as an experiment in ecumenism that is bearing fruit!

Combatting Racism in Europe

There are approximately 20 million migrants and refugees in Europe today with an estimated two million additional clandestine or undocumented migrant workers. These figures do not take into account the hundreds of thousands of displaced persons caught in civil strife in their own countries in the Balkans. In the struggle against racism, anti-Semitism and xenophobia, the 1989 European Ecumenical Assembly in Basel stated that as Churches and Christians "we are called to include the minorities which stand out against pressure for their assimilation, and plead for the dignity for those who are marginalized...The European house should be an 'open house,' a place of refuge and protection, a place of welcome, a place of hospitality."

However, since 1989 there has been a steady increase in the number of attacks on the Romany (Gypsies) in Slovakia and Romania, on Turks and Kurds in Germany, on Vietnamese workers in Eastern Europe, on North Africans in France, on Sri Lankans wherever they seek asylum, and on persons of color in almost every country. While some attacks are verbal, many more are violent and have included setting fire to homes of asylum seekers, and physically attacking foreigners on trains and trams or even in clubs where they gather for social occasions. Some of these attacks are led by "skinheads" and neo-nazi groups but a general xenophobia pervades much of Europe today and, with the raising of barriers and the closing of borders to newcomers, gives rise to the image of "Fortress Europe."

Fifteen men and women from seven countries in central and eastern Europe attended the second Training Seminar for Ecumenical Refugee Work during August and September 1994. The participants came from Estonia, Moldova, Ukraine, Russia, Romania, Serbia and Croatia. This course, under the auspices of the Conference of European Churches, enabled the trainees to study at first hand the work of the churches in reception and protection of refugees and asylum seekers. They considered not only political and legal factors, but also pastoral and humanitarian responses which are challenging the churches.

In May 1994, the archbishop of Canterbury issued the following "Statement on Racism," which was cosigned by more than sixty Orthodox, Catholic, Old Catholic, Anglican, and Protestant church leaders—patriarchs, archbishops, moderators, presidents, and chairpersons—from twenty European countries. The statement is a challenge to the churches of Europe, but, with wide media coverage, it also reached and was heard by the general public.

European Church Leaders' Statement On Racism

Christian people in Europe have been able to welcome the breaking down of barriers and the liberating possibilities which have been brought about by the collapse of totalitarian regimes in Eastern Europe. There are, however, some new causes for alarm. As church leaders, we view with the very gravest concern the rise of racism, xenophobia and anti-Semitism in all European countries. We are troubled about the unequal treatment given to those of different social or ethnic origin. We are especially disturbed, indeed outraged, by the growth of harassment and violence directed against such people. Every attack of this kind is an attack on one who is made in the image of God. We declare our solidarity with those threatened or molested, in the name of Christ who himself became human.

The variety of cultural and religious traditions which belong historically to Europe are part of a rich heritage which Christians acknowledge and celebrate. We reject any suggestion of superiority or movement towards exclusiveness which would deprive others of a place in the new Europe, whether they have been here for some time, have a human right to enter or have sought safety from persecution or conflict.

Racism—the assumption of superiority and the exercise of dominant power against those of different ethnic background—is a sin. We call on all Christians, and we invite those of other faith communities, to work to eradicate racism from ourselves, our churches, our countries and our continent. This process should be carried out in the spheres of housing, health, employment, immigration and refuge policy, and all other relevant areas.

We recognize there may be a cost, in resources needed and criticism to be endured. However this is a requirement of God's mission. As followers of Jesus Christ we can offer nothing less.

World Student Federation Celebrating 100 Years

1995 marks the centennial anniversary of the World Student Christian Federation (WSCF), which was established in 1895 at Vadstena Castle, Sweden, by students and student leaders from ten North American and European countries.

Many ecumenical giants had their roots in the WSCF. John R. Mott and Francis Pickens Miller of the United States, W. A. Visser 't Hooft of the Netherlands, D. T. Niles of Ceylon (Sri Lanka), K. H. Ting of China, Philip Potter of Dominica (West Indies), and Madeleine Barot and Suzanne de Diétrich of France were among the architects of the federation. Most students today do not know these names nor have much interest in the federation's history. But in the late summer of 1995 in the Ivory Coast city of Yamoussoukro, far from the castle of Vadstena, the federation will celebrate its centennial as a "Community of Memory and Hope."

Throughout Europe, as in the United States, the student rebellions of the late sixties had a powerful but negative effect on the Student Christian Movements. Individualism reigned and all structures were called into question. In the past five years, however, the SCMs in Europe have taken on new life and vitality. Today, there are at least twenty-nine national movements from Austria to Spain, Belarus to Slovakia, Great Britain to Russia.

In a recent issue of *Mozaik*, the journal of the European Region of the World Student Christian Federation, Torsten Moritz of its editorial team writes that "the growth of the federation after the end of the Cold War era has changed the face of the federation. This change is confronting us with new tasks. Coming from the East and the West, as Orthodox or Protestants from very different spiritual traditions, we have to accept how different we are. This requires a lot of tolerance, a willingness to learn about one another, lots of patience and an attitude of 'listening first.'

"Talking about 'multicultural awareness' and seeing multicultural societies as a promising perspective, we have to come to terms with the fact that our federation is quite multicultural itself. We therefore should see the debate and the doubts about ecumenism in WSCF as an important and valuable chance to get into an exchange. . . . The most important question will be whether we'll be able to carry on with active involvement in the process of changing the face of Europe or whether we will turn into a self-centered bunch of people."

American churches join the federation in its celebration through prayer and solidarity, remembering that "many clusters of Christian students are meeting in the setting of an unbroken history of one hundred years, a period marked by courage, vision, commitment, and action. They become part of a heritage in which the study of the Bible and the struggle to understand the meaning of the Gospel leads them to dare to challenge some of the fundamental assumptions of society and the church." We must listen to their voices as we and they seek to remember the future.

Young adults from United Christian Fellowship in Burgos, Spain, do street evangelism on Saturday night on the Promenade

Latin Europe

Paolo Naso

Protestant Identity in Latin Europe

Being a Significant Minority

To outline the situation of the churches in Latin Europe (Belgium, France, Portugal, Spain, Italy, and certain regions of Switzerland) is challenging, because "Latin Europe" is not a geopolitical area at all. Some regions of Italy and France, for example, are fully integrated into the world's most economically developed areas; other regions, such as areas of Portugal, are struggling towards modernization. There are even striking cultural and political fault lines within the single states as, for example, between central and southern Italy, or between Andalusia and Catalonia in Spain.

Latin Europe is a mosaic of well-differentiated subcultures. One dominant historical and cultural factor, however, links the several nations: the fact that all are marked by a pervasive Catholic heritage. The Conference of Protestant Churches in Latin Europe, in fact, was launched in pre-Vatican II times as a strategy to strengthen defensive minority churches and their interests in democratizing society in lands with massive Catholic experience.

The presumed "Christian identity" in Latin Europe is long on heritage but short on practiced commitment. This identity has been described as "a la carte" Christianity, where it is possible to choose from spiritual goods in a spirit of individualistic convenience. Likewise it has been called a "faith patchwork," combining elements from different religious traditions. The dominant characteristic for all is a secularization of the faith experience.

Italy is a striking example: In 1974 and 1981 the majority of the electorate, which had long followed the line of the Catholic party, voted, respectively, to recognize divorce and legalize abortion, turning aside the intense campaign of the national Conference of Catholic Bishops and confirming the fact that the pope, while celebrated, is increasingly less followed.

Consider this paradox: At one time Europe was the Christian continent; here entire lands converted to Christianity; here were launched crusades and missionaries to "Christianize" distant places; here the Reformation and Counter Reformation generated alternative ways to approach spiritual and public life, modernity, liberties, and rights. However, the enduring portion for Latin Europe would be the experience of

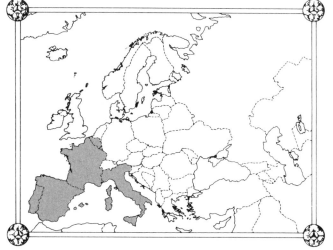

19

the Counter Reformation, which was inhospitable to religious pluralism, enlightened government, and the practice of science. Secularization overtook even the conservative bastions of Latin Europe.

Minority snapshots

In France, with a nominally Catholic population, the Federation of Protestant Churches—including Lutheran, Reformed, Baptist and Pentecostal bodies—embraces a constituency of one million persons. The generally positive image of Protestants in the country is sustained by surveys finding that an additional number, roughly equal to the actual number of Protestants, considers itself "close" to the Protestant experience. The Orthodox community numbers some 400,000 persons. However, today, in this land of Huguenots, there are more Muslims than Protestants, a fact that has changed the religious ethos in many areas.

Italian Protestants in the "shadow of the Vatican" number about half a million, most belonging to Pentecostal churches, while some 50,000 belong to the historical denominations (Waldensian-Methodist, Baptist, Lutheran) related to the national Federation of Protestant Churches, which also includes the Salvation Army and some independent congregations. The Federation, based in Rome, carries on important social and educational ministries, including weekly radio and bi-weekly television programs. The Federation and related denominations are generally marked with a spirituality that binds biblical faith, political conscience, and public responsibility. Agape, the Protestant conference and retreat center in the mountains of northern Italy, is known throughout the world for its international conferences and ecumenical work camp programs.

An Assembly of Gypsies

For centuries, Gypsies in Europe have been victims of racism and oppression. Many were rounded up by the Nazis and died in extermination camps. They are still an unwanted people in many cities and countries. Recognizing no national borders, the Gypsies wander across Europe from Romania to Spain. However, in France, the Evangelical Mission of Gypsies of France organizes a great assembly each year. In August 1994, 40,000 Gypsies in 8,000 caravans descended upon the small village of Damblain, France, spending several days at the nearby former military base. The conference, organized over many months, received thousands of evangelical Protestant and Pentecostal Gypsies from different groups, coming from all parts of Europe for prayer, Bible study, and to encounter the members of the "larger family" scattered across Europe. The Evangelical Gypsy Mission is a member of the Protestant Federation of France and has about 80,000 baptized members and 850 pastors, lay preachers and evangelists.

Protestants in Spain number some 90,000, mostly Brethren and Baptists of a strongly pietistic spirituality, a smaller but socially active Spanish Evangelical Church (Presbyterian and Methodist), and an Episcopal Church. The latter two churches have a united theological seminary in Madrid. In 1492, when the last Muslim forces were defeated and the Jewish community was expelled from Spain, all non-Catholic religions were outlawed until 1868, when religious tolerance was recognized constitutionally. Effectively, however, religious freedom was not to have its way until a full century later.

In Portugal there are some 50,000 Protestants, mostly Presbyterians, Methodists, and Lusitanians. The Lusitanian Catholic-Apostolic Evangelical Church is in communion with the Church of England. These churches belong to the Council of Christian Churches, which focuses upon educational programming and church growth. From the overthrow of Portugal's civilian government in 1926, through the fascist dictatorship of Prime Minister Salazar, and until the 1974 Revolution, the country's Protestants suffered severe repression.

In Belgium, the Protestant churches are a small minority often divided into the two language groups characteristic of the nation. Flemish, a Dutch dialect, is the official language of Flanders in the North, while French is official in the South. The United Protestant Church of Belgium was created by bringing together the Methodists and Reformed communities. With Brussels as the capital of the European Union, there is a strong international ecumenical presence through the work of the European Ecumenical Commission on Church and Society.

In Switzerland, French-speaking Protestant cantons like Geneva, Vaud, and Neuchatel have had a dynamic Protestant presence that has permeated the Protestantism of Latin Europe. The Federation of Swiss Protestant Churches has given strong moral, economic, and pastoral support to sister churches in neighboring countries. Since the Reformation, many Swiss pastors have served pastorates in Belgium and France.

In all the Latin Europe countries, despite harsh, even repressive Counter Reformation experiences, significant Protestant minorities developed and have survived to model and to open up space for freedom, democratic pluralism, and multi-ethnic and multicultural life.

Dialogue limited

With some notable exceptions, official dialogue with the Catholic Church, particularly with the bishops, has been a troubled affair. France alone manages regular high-level inter-confessional consultations. In Spain and Portugal the scene is bleak, with the Protestants inhibited by defensive mentalities and the Catholics still clinging in too many cases to pre-Vatican II ecumenical positions. Through its relations with the Council of European Bishops' Conferences, the Conference of European Churches is one forum where minority communities can be heard and their needs expressed.

In Italy, there is an arresting story at the grass roots level. Although the Pentecostal churches tend to stay to themselves, the Federation-related denominations are deeply committed to ecumenical exchange through Bible study and through initiatives of the World Council of

Buying a watercolor of Notre Dame Cathedral in Paris

Worker Priests

In the fall of 1993 the commission on labor of the Roman Catholic Church in France officially recognized the contribution of "worker priests" and apologized to those who suffered from a 1954 decision to end that experiment. (After Cardinal Roncalli became Pope John XXIII in 1958, he relaxed the ban on worker priests.)

The statement marked the fiftieth anniversary of the publication of the book *France: Land of Mission?*, widely credited with giving birth to the worker priest movement, though it does not explicitly use that term. Two chaplains from the Young Christian Workers movement, Henri Godin and Yvan Daniel, wrote the book in 1943 to address the growing gap between the "dechristianized masses" and the Christian community.

The worker priest movement was born when four priests asked for permission to seek secular jobs as a way of getting to know the workers and their world. The archbishop of Paris approved the request. But traditional circles reacted swiftly with protests to the Vatican, and in 1954 a hundred French worker priests were abruptly ordered to leave their workplaces and return to traditional priestly functions. Most made the painful decision to abandon their jobs, but some felt obliged to continue their mission and broke with the church.

Saying that "the wounds created by the 1954 decision are not yet closed," the commission on labor assured those priests "that we recognize that they were seeking to be faithful to their mission."

The commission said the growing number of religious involved today in the workaday world, which is increasingly vulnerable to "new poverty, new precariousness, and new exclusions," are demonstrating God's preferential love for the poor and the truth that Jesus came for all.

An article in the French Catholic monthly *L'Actualité religieuse dans le monde* puts the present number of worker priests at 570 in France, 130 in Italy, 80 in Spain, 35 in Belgium, and 15 in Germany.

—excerpted from *One World*, December 1993

The CIMADE:
Conscience of a Nation

One of the best known church-related institutions in Europe is the CIMADE, created in 1939 by Protestant and Orthodox youth movements, with strong support and leadership from the French Reformed and Lutheran Churches. It was led for many years by the indomitable, imaginative, and fearless Madeleine Barot. (CIMADE is an acronym coming from the French name, Comité Inter-Mouvements Auprès Des Evacués).

From 1940 to 1944, Jews of French nationality, Gypsies, Jewish refugees from Germany and Austria, non-Jewish opponents to fascism from these same areas, and refugees from Spain who had fled their country at the end of the civil war, were interned in camps and finally turned over to the Nazis by the Vichy Government. Later they were sent to Germany where a large number of them died in concentration camps. CIMADE team members went to live inside the camps in France, providing support and distribution of supplies received mainly from abroad. They soon started to organize a network of escape routes, in particular to Switzerland.

Madeleine Barot has written that "life behind barbed wire was an adventure. Clandestineness was another. All adventure brings risks. Those that we ran were in every way less serious than those faced by our Jewish friends. How could we be present among them if we had not also taken spiritual and physical risks?" After the war, the CIMADE received fraternal workers from abroad to assist in relief work in France and with its former enemy, Germany, constantly working for reconciliation. Later, it also initiated significant development projects in African nations where France had had colonial ties, as well as in Haiti and Nicaragua.

The Reverend Jacques Maury, CIMADE's president, recently described the CIMADE as being "on the cutting edge of a complacent society, always looking for meaning, asking the difficult questions of both the citizens of France and the French Government, giving a witness of solidarity to those who are rejected or unjustly treated—refugees, asylum seekers, and particularly immigrants from Northern Africa." Its actions today are centered on reconciliation, healing, welcoming, and sharing.

In a recent action, it challenged the French government to reestablish full compliance with the Convention of Geneva regarding the rights of refugees and asylum seekers whose lives are at risk by expulsion from France. The concentration camps are gone but the CIMADE is at work in "retention centers" where persons at risk are now being held prior to being expelled from the country. CIMADE, a David among the Goliaths of France, remains a strong voice for justice, compassion, and human rights as it seeks to follow the challenge of Micah 6:8: "What does the Lord require of you but to do justice, and to love kindness, and to walk humbly with your God?"

Churches' program on Justice, Peace, and the Integrity of Creation with Catholic base communities, the latter very often critical of the Catholic hierarchy. A bright sign is an ecumenical faith and culture monthly, *Confronti*, published jointly by Protestant Federation-related persons and Catholic base communities.

At the denominational level, a first-ever venture in Italy, an official joint team from the Waldensian-Methodist Synod and the Catholic Conference of Bishops recently issued for review a draft statement on the critical issue of mixed marriages. Also to be noted is the post-Vatican II Ecumenical Activities Secretariat, which promotes year-round local ecumenical workshops and a national summertime conference drawing some 500 Catholic and Protestant leaders.

Selective ecumenism

What is ahead ecumenically in Italy is hard to say. For Catholics, the presence of the Vatican keeps attention on the pope rather than on the local church. We must underscore the point, however, that at the local level and on specific issues such as solidarity with immigrants and refugees, the continuing struggles against racism and the Mafia culture, and support for a multi-cultural, multi-ethnic, pluralistic society, there are increasing instances of common engagement, called "selective ecumenism" by some Protestants.

With the exception of France, Catholic church-state relations were highlighted in national constitutions or in concordats with the devastating consequence that until very recent decades other religious groups had to endure severe discrimination. Spain's expulsion of the Jews in 1492 cast a long shadow over religious freedom for any non-Catholic people. It was not until after the death of General Franco in 1975 and the reestablishment of democracy in Spain that the Spanish Parliament declared non-discrimination the national policy in 1978.

Likewise in Portugal, until 1975, the Catholic religion was regarded as the religion of the state. There was no constitutional freedom of religion. Non-Catholic constituencies had to meet state requirements to be recognized at all, and in any case they could not engage in social action or cultural activities. The climate changed radically following the Revolution of 1974. Freedom of religion was established, and, for example, the Portugese Presbyterian Church could transform and enlarge its conference center at Figueira de Foz, placing it at the service of the ecumenical community.

A situation clearly apart is that of France, where the Revolution of 1789 opened the way for a secular state that recognizes the exercise of religion in a manner fully independent of the state. It is not by chance that the visibility of the Protestant minority in its social and cultural dimensions is considerable, and in fact exceeds what its numbers might otherwise enjoy. Developing in full stride with other aspects of a secular and pluralistic state, Protestants took an active role in the building of a modern middle class-driven society, with the Third Republic (1870-1914) as the "golden age" for French

We Dare to Resist

From the courageous declaration of the Waldensian and Baptist Churches in Palermo, adopted by an assembly in Riesi of the Waldensian and Methodist churches in Sicily, the day following the 23 May 1992 assassination of Giovanni Falcone, chief state prosecutor against the Mafia forces in Italy.

We believe in the God to whom Jesus pointed, who brings low the mighty and sustains the humble.

We resist the belief that either you are afraid or you make others afraid. We want to believe that finding the courage to resist and sharing the courage to persevere are possible.

We believe that in Jesus, a Jew, a Palestinian carpenter in whom dwelt the fullness of God and the Spirit of truth and justice—in this Jesus we find the way through. He alone is Lord!

With him we choose to resist the death forces, believing that it is not "either ourselves or others," but that evil can be resisted, the Mafia overcome and tribute no longer paid to "either silence or death."

We believe in the gift of the Spirit of God, the backbone of our resistance, our strength in times of defeat, our courage to stand up to oppression. The Spirit is our guide!

With the Spirit we condemn any who spill blood and take the law into their own hands, who resort to violence, who corrupt others and let themselves be corrupted.

With the Spirit we care to believe that the flowers of our fields and streets where our children play no longer will be stained by the blood of the innocent and of the evil, because the last word cries out for life.

Fr. Giuseppe Puglisi, murdered by the Mafia on 15 December 1993, his 57th birthday

Drug rehabilitation center near Burgos, Spain, operated by United Christian Fellowship

diaspora is authentic, yeasty ferment, each making its significant difference for justice and radical pluralism across a broadly diversified and ever-changing global, social, religious, and cultural space which some dare call ecumenopolis." Its evangelistic outreach will be its life blood!

Dr. Paolo Naso, a member of the Waldensian Church, is director of the ecumenical magazine Confronti. *The author of books on social problems in southern Italy and the Christian community in Israel and Palestine, he recently edited a book of writings by Martin Luther King that had previously been unknown to the Italian public.*

Protestantism. There was danger here, of course, in that Protestant identity could easily fall into a conventional, secularized way of life, which is why French Protestant thinkers called for the churches to be active and high-profile critics of the state where the latter's moral and social vision was at variance with Christian values.

In Latin Europe, still marked by a powerful Catholic presence, relations between church and state remain a critical element in the struggle to assure that religious minorities can breath freely, witness openly, and practice their faith without undo restrictions.

Ferment in diaspora

Clearly the last several decades have opened up broad new ranges for religious pluralism in Latin Europe. Minority groups, though they must be ever-vigilant, do have a new lease on freedom of action. National policies now effectively view the several religious and cultural minorities as precious components in the complex identity of each land. The search is on by the states and religious bodies alike to negotiate a new architecture of community that affirms and safeguards cultural and religious pluralism.

Islam in Europe is claiming its rightful space in nations heretofore popularly regarded as "Christian." In France, Muslims outnumber French Huguenots. Civil governments are being forced to wrestle with complicated issues related to religious freedom and the rise of Islamic fundamentalism, not only in France but in Germany and the United Kingdom. In England it is estimated that there are more Sikhs than Baptists, more Hindus than Methodists, and more Muslims than Baptists, Methodists, and Presbyterians combined.

In this light, a useful paradigm for Protestant minority identity increasingly appears to be that of diaspora. As Frank Gibson of the American Waldensian Society has written, "Within a secularized context

Northern Europe

Tom Dorris

Scandinavia and the Baltics

Compared to other areas of Europe, Christianity came to modern-day Scandinavia and the Baltic countries relatively late, although still several centuries before Europeans settled in North America. (The term "Scandinavia" usually refers to the countries of Norway, Sweden, and Denmark, although it can also include Finland and Iceland. It is used here in its most inclusive meaning.) Often the new faith came in the context of battle and bloodshed, though Icelanders (who are already making plans to celebrate 1,000 years of Christianity on their island at the end of this century), are pleased to note that in their case Christianity was accepted peacefully after a debate and majority vote in the parliament of the time. Members in favor of retaining the Norse gods were not forced into waters nearby for immediate baptism after the parliamentary decision, as was the case in other places. Instead, they were allowed to postpone the rite until they could hike to warmer waters fed by one of Iceland's many thermal springs.

The Reformation carried with it virtually the entire population of northern Europe. As a result, Lutheranism is by far the numerically dominant Christian communion in this region. (The Baltic nation of Lithuania is one notable exception; most of its Christians are Roman Catholics.) Not surprisingly, the Lutheran Church is the official state church in all the Scandinavian countries, as well as the largest single church in both Latvia and Estonia, which were once parts of the Swedish Empire. Small numbers of Roman Catholics also exist in Scandinavia, composed mainly of refugees, immigrants, and local converts from the state church. Members of other Protestant denominations, "free churches" as they are known (for example, Methodist, Missionary Covenant, and Baptist), are scattered throughout Scandinavia and the Baltics. Their members are descendants of converts from various eighteenth- and nineteenth-century revival movements.

The fluid and permeable boundary between Eastern and Western Christianity passes through parts of northern Europe as well. Thus, though Christianity in its Western form is overwhelmingly prevalent in the region, there is a small, but disproportionately influential, community of indigenous Eastern Orthodox Christians. This is most notable in Finland, where both the 60,000-member Finnish Orthodox Church

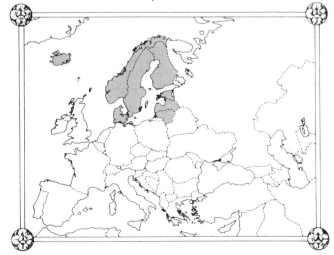

and the 4.6 million-member Finnish Lutheran Church have equal status as state churches. In several countries of the region, the Eastern Christian presence has increased in recent decades, chiefly because of the arrival of refugees and immigrants.

In much of the region, the Reformation caused relatively little disruption to the structures of church life. Entire dioceses, including their bishops, simply withdrew from the Church of Rome. Although considered a defining era in church history, northern Europeans do not regard the Reformation as a total break with the past. In no way is the change from Roman Catholicism to Lutheranism in the sixteenth century understood as the beginning of a "new" church. Rather, to take Sweden as an example, the (Lutheran) Church of Sweden is considered to be simply the principal modern manifestation of the church in Sweden, in continuity with a Christian community whose roots in the land can be traced back for more than a thousand years.

In North America, institutional expressions of Christianity have multiplied—in the form of denominations and independent, parachurch organizations based on race, social status, theological beliefs, ethnic heritage, and worship styles. Religious groups have no special legal status, nor ability to teach in public schools. Rather, church-state separation and financial support by member contributions are the norm.

Christians in northern Europe, however, experience the church in quite another form. The overwhelming majority of the population belongs to the same church, known variously as the national, folk, or state church. Rich and poor, educated or less educated, local or immigrant, groups that are divergent in their theology and personal piety—groups that would have gone separate denominational ways in North

America—can and do remain together, at least nominally, in one state church.

Within the uniting umbrella of the state church, individual belief and practice tends to be treated as a very private matter. Many church members feel it quite natural to pick and choose in terms of the elements that together form their personal faith and piety, regardless of "official" church teachings. The services and hymns heard in the state churches of northern Europe will be familiar to anyone who has attended a Lutheran service in North America. However, unlike North America, any given parish within the state churches of northern Europe often will include evangelicals, theological liberals, theological conservatives, social activists, charismatics, pietists, and agnostics as members of the same congregation.

Although there is complete freedom of religious belief, the national church of each state enjoys a special legal status different from other, smaller, religious organizations. It has the right to collect federal, provincial, and local tax money for its activities. The state church may hold religion classes in public schools as part of the general curriculum. Church holidays are all state holidays. The state church has easy access to state-controlled media, including regular TV and radio programs. In turn, the state is involved with certain functions of the church. For example, it has been common for the elected government to officially appoint the bishops of the national church (although at the time of this writing the Swedish government was considering a proposal from the church to name its own bishops).

This unique national or folk ethos of the Scandinavian churches leads many northern Europeans to treat the state church as if it were just another public service—like the post office, the fire department or the telephone company—or even to

---

A Story of Swedish Ecumenism

The Church of Sweden and the Swedish Methodist Church have entered into an agreement of cooperation that is unique, according to a report from the Church of Sweden information service. The agreement says that there is full communion of proclamation and sacraments between the two churches and that the validity of the ordination of pastors and elders is recognized. The churches retain their organizational independence. A council for cooperation between the two churches is being set up. It will be the council's task to ensure that the agreement penetrates to the local congregations of the two churches. The Swedish Methodist Church has about five thousand members, while the Church of Sweden—the world's largest Lutheran church—has over 7.6 million members.

—Lutheran World Information 15/94

think of it as a government agency for spiritual matters. And yet many who would never think of becoming actively involved in church life—who never join in public worship, who would not consider church teachings as guides for daily life—are, at the same time, in some vague way, glad that the folk church continues to exist. Although they may have very little contact with it beyond formal occasions, a great number of northern Europeans would be uncomfortable in a society from which the state church would be absent. Thus, although church-state ties are loosening, there is no significant support in northern Europe for a complete divorce.

Low attendance

It is commonplace to describe northern Europe as a highly secularized part of the world, and in many ways this is an accurate reflection of the situation—especially, for instance, if one compares church attendance in the region with that in the United States. More than forty percent of the people in the United States claim to attend church regularly. In Scandinavia less than five percent do. (The situation in the Baltic republics, compounded by decades of official atheism and oppression of the churches during the period of Soviet rule, is still unclear.)

And yet, paradoxically, there are ways in which the church is more present, or at least more noticed, in secular northern Europe society than in the United States. Above all, there is a heightened sense in the state churches of northern Europe that the folk church is the church for

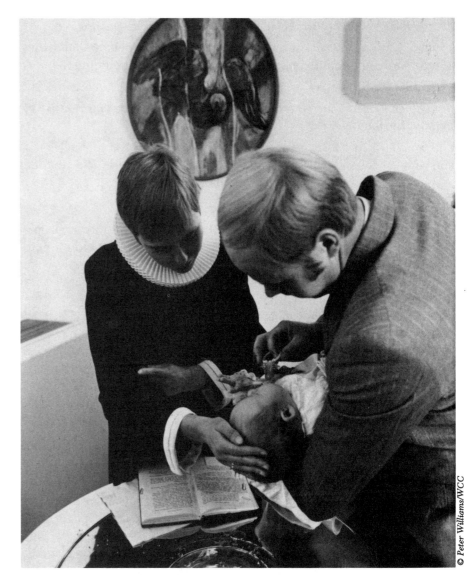

Baptism with Pastor Litten Hjorth in church at Over Hadsten, Denmark

Interview with Ivo Grantins

Ivo Grantins is Latvian. Born in 1969, he was baptized at 17 and ordained a priest four years later in 1991. Since then, he has been pastor of a Lutheran parish of about 250 people in the northern Latvian town of Rujiena. When interviewed in mid-1994, he had just completed the first year of a projected three-year study leave in Sweden. He will work in his parish during summers, and is able to visit on occasion during the rest of the year.

You chose to be baptized as a 17-year-old, in a society where such a decision was certainly not officially encouraged. How did that happen?

I was unsatisfied with official teachings and philosophies. I was critical, and looking for different values. There was only one officially allowed worldview at the time. Wherever you went you met it.

Joining the church then probably didn't help your career possibilities.

Of course not, but the church was a place where a person could find things more important than a career. I think many of my contemporaries weren't so interested in a career in such a society.

How do you evaluate what happened to the church in the half century of communist rule?

The wonder is that it survived, especially when you look at the collaboration with the state, the low attendance, and the few converts. We are used to vegetating, and I hope we can overcome that.

How did things change with Latvian independence in 1991?

During the struggle for independence, I had never seen so many people in church, and so many praying people, even though they didn't quite know how to behave in church. And politicians and media people were using phrases like "God only knows," and "only God can help us." Now we seem to be approaching some Third World countries in social structure, with a very few rich people and not much of a middle class. Instead of communist materialism, some people are turning to capitalist materialism, and their values are now measured in dollars or cars or gold. Now a whole other world has opened, with possibilities to make lots of money. That is one obstacle to people coming to the church. Now, with independence, we receive responsibility, which we didn't have in Soviet times, when we could blame it all on "the Russians" or "Asiatic culture" or something. Some people are losing hope right now because independence didn't give all what people expected.

How do people in Latvia today react to people who are Christians?

It is still so that some people, especially in the intelligentsia, say that to be religious is to be a non-thinking person. And even among people in general, if you tell them you are a Christian, never mind being a priest, they become stiff, and think that if you are Christian that means you claim to be a saint, and they think they have to behave in some different way towards you.

What are some of the problems the church in Latvia faces in the post-communist period?

There are so many problems that we cannot manage them. There is a big lack of professional workers in the church. There are so many opportunities right now that we can't answer them. We see that no one is working with the poor. And many people are coming to the church for religious instruction. And we have the opportunity to teach religion in schools, but we don't have qualified teachers to send. We have received back our church property, and we can do nothing with it. We don't have people skilled in property management. I want to cry when I see it—how much it is possible to do, and how few things we are able to do.

What major concerns do you have for your church and country in the next few years?

My big hope is that the past will not come back, that the Russians will not come back. Somebody who has been on a sinking boat is always a bit nervous about any boat after that. This experience is so strong, that for me it is quite realistic that it could happen.

the whole nation. At its best such an attitude means that church leaders somehow feel responsible for the whole country: for all its people (church members or not, active or not), its natural resources, its social and political policies, and its economic programs.

Speaking out

Statements by folk church leaders in northern Europe tend to get more public attention and to cover a wider spectrum of issues than statements by church leaders in the United States. Refugee policy, transportation priorities, foreign aid, and whether to recognize homosexual partnerships, are actual examples of issues in northern Europe on which church leaders have spoken in recent years. This in no way should be understood, however, to mean that individuals, society as a whole, or the government in particular, will actually follow the advice these leaders offer!

Sometimes these paradoxical aspects of Christianity in northern Europe appear in the most unexpected contexts. In the 1994 Finnish presidential election campaign, candidate Elisabeth Rehn, in response to a question from a voter about her personal faith, said that she had no proof of the historical existence of Jesus. Rehn emphasized, however, that she considered herself a devout Christian. Her comments about Jesus' existence prompted intense media, church, and academic reaction, although less than five percent of the Finnish population attends church regularly. One could not say that this was the issue upon which the election turned, but Rehn's opponent, Martii Ahtisaari, himself a former member of the Finnish Lutheran Church's foreign affairs council, made it clear that he believed "what the Lutheran Church in Finland taught." Ahtisaari won.

The Baltic States

Although one can still find something of a dominant folk church mentality in the three Baltic countries of Lithuania, Latvia, and Estonia, the half century of occupation of these lands by the former Soviet Union (1941-1989) means that no one church is established by law in these lands. It also means that each of the large national Lutheran churches in Estonia and Latvia has a counterpart Lutheran church in exile, which exists among those who left their homeland during the Soviet occupation. Since the collapse of communism and the renewal of the independence of the Baltic states, these "exile" and "home" churches are struggling to reestablish ties after 50 years of deep antagonism.

Methodist and Reformed churches are also present in the Baltic states, as well as Baptists and Pentecostals.

Dominant issues

From the end of the Second World War until the end of communist rule in Russia (1945-1989), issues of disarmament and the East-West confrontation have been major concerns of the Scandinavian churches. In 1983 Scandinavian church leaders convened a Christian World Conference on Life in Peace in Uppsala, Sweden. It brought

Baltic Lutherans Address Consequences of Occupation

"Consequences of the Soviet Occupation and Challenges to the Churches" was the theme of a consultation in Norway organized by the Lutheran World Federation for Lutheran church leaders from Estonia, Latvia, and Lithuania in September 1994. Excerpts from their communiqué are given below.

One of the heaviest heritages left by the occupation has been the large-scale systematic distortion of the demographic pattern of the Baltic states. Planned migratory waves of people from the Soviet Union, deportations and forced exile and killings of the native populations have brought the populations, particularly in Latvia and Estonia, almost to the point of becoming minorities in their own countries. Issues of citizenship and residence laws, full respect and safeguarding of human rights of all the inhabitants, minority and cultural autonomy matters confront the Baltic states and their authorities with gigantic challenges. Here as well the international community needs to gain a more thorough and proper understanding of the facts, history and dynamics of the Baltic situation in order to fulfill an adequate role of critical solidarity, promote positive solutions and avoid an escalation of existing problems.

Fifty years of occupation have caused heavy ecological damage, both through military presence and activities as well as destructive economic exploitation.

Equally, if not more worrying, is the spiritual and ethical damage done to the human beings through fifty years of imposed ideological indoctrination and isolation. Issues of responsibility and tolerance are of great actuality. The past atheistic propaganda has also produced a great number of people without any positive attitude to Christian faith and laid the ground for superstition and new religious movements.

Called by the gospel, the church has a responsibility to care for the entire society and people among whom it lives and ministers…In spite of shortcomings, the churches in the Baltic countries are fully determined to face their responsibilities and seek to serve the society, alone and in cooperation with the authorities and all persons of good will. But, especially at this stage, these churches stand in great need of accompaniment and solidarity. They appeal to the ecumenical fellowship and the international community not to be forgotten and left alone at this most crucial stage when they and the people they serve are geared toward the task of fully recovering independence, democracy, and full human dignity for all persons, regardless of their origins or background.

together representatives from churches around the world, and led to the formation of a special research center to consider issues of peace and justice from a global church perspective. (Due to the Soviet occupation, Baltic churches were less free to act independently on such issues.)

Today, Christians in the North are deeply concerned about issues of social justice. In the Scandinavian countries, as decades of public commitment to a social democratic approach to society are under review or even threat, the church may find itself called upon to shoulder more of society's commitment to protect and support those less well off, such as the unemployed and the sick. It may also find its official stance politically unpopular on such things as the rights of refugees and immigrants. Besides issues related to new arrivals, it has also begun to pay more sympathetic attention to its indigenous minority membership, notably the Sami peoples (Lapps) in northern Norway, Sweden, and Finland, and Greenlanders (whose ecclesiastical autonomy as a separate diocese is now officially recognized.)

After major restrictions on its life and work during the half century of communist rule, the church in the Baltics finds itself confronted by demands for many types of ministry (in education and social work, for instance), but it lacks recent experience, trained personnel, financial resources, and a functioning infrastructure to make an adequate response. It must also minister in the midst of another difficult legacy of Soviet times—significant portions of the population whose ethnic identity and language are other than Estonian, Latvian, or Lithuanian.

Ecumenism

Ecumenism too has been a major concern of Christians in northern Europe. Several prominent ecumenical figures over the years have come from the Scandinavian countries. Perhaps the most noted is Nathan Soderblöm, former archbishop of Uppsala from World War I until the early 1930s. Soderblöm took the lead in convening the 1925 Stockholm Conference on issues of life and work. The subsequent Life and Work movement became one of the predecessors of the World Council of Churches. Soderblöm was also active in the other major forerunner of the WCC, the Faith and Order movement.

Continuing influence

Through active missions in North America in the nineteenth century, and in Africa and Asia in this century, the folk churches of northern Europe have passed the gospel on to generations of non-Europeans. Through their cultures as well, a strong Christian witness is maintained in their lands and throughout the world. For example, two nineteenth-century Danes whose writings continue to have a wide influence are the philosopher Søren Kierkegaard, and the hymnographer and author N.F.S. Grundtvig, many of whose hymns continue to be sung regularly throughout Protestant churches in North America. Even the small Orthodox Christian community exerts an important influence through its liturgical reforms and throughout the worldwide Orthodox Christian communion.

The Passion hymns of Hallgrimur Petersson, composed more than 300 years ago, are considered national treasures in Iceland. Commonly read aloud in homes, and broadcast on Icelandic radio after the evening news during Lent, they witness to the special ethos of Christianity in the secular lands of northern Europe. With their strong cadences, national emphasis, universal perspective, and with a simple piety often found in remote areas, they form a fitting conclusion to this brief review of the folk Christianity in northern Europe:

God grant that in my mother tongue
Your gospel may be sounded
To rich and poor, to old and young,
Its blessing be expounded.
Over vale and glen, by lip and pen,
To each remotest dwelling,
While your strong hands safeguard our land,
Dangers and foes repelling.

Tom Dorris was a deacon of the Evangelical Lutheran Church in America (ELCA), serving as communications director for the Life and Peace Institute in Uppsala, Sweden. He was killed in a car accident in July 1994.

© Peter Williams/WCC

Central Europe

Werner Krusche

The Experience of Protestant Churches in East Germany

In February 1991, fifteen months after the fall of the Berlin Wall, the East German Federation of Protestant Churches was dissolved and the unification of the Evangelical Church in Germany, East and West, took place later that spring. This article is excerpted from Bishop Krusche's address to that final meeting of the Federation. —*Editor*

In all probability, this will be our last meeting as a Federal Synod. We would part without dignity and gratitude if we left without looking back, as if our Federation belonged to the "scrapheap of history," as apparentlyso many things in the German Democratic Republic (GDR) do, as if it had been nothing but a makeshift solution to be thrown out abruptly and painlessly, and we had to return to normality as quickly as possible. But the opposite is true: It is extremely appropriate to take a thorough look back and to analyze how our common journey has affected us and those around us.

Looking back we do by no means intend to gild and nostalgically transfigure the past. We are too much aware of our mistakes and errors and the instances when we did not trust God to help us and in not doing so heaped guilt upon ourselves. By no means shall we lay aside these years as a time lost in which we applied our best energies to something unworthy of our efforts. We lived through that period intensively, we gathered insights and experience with the living God and with each other. It is not true to say that we always felt depressed, heavy laden, timid, embittered, hopeless—as some, and sometimes we ourselves, tried to tell us. We did not only suffer, groan, and hurt. We also celebrated, rejoiced, laughed together, felt free, expanded our imagination, encouraged each other. We must not pretend that all this did not happen, although we church people must confess that we had it easier in many ways than our brothers and sisters in secular professions.

We did not start our journey through those years at our own will. We traveled a path to which God led us and on which God gave us guidance. Nobody need criticize us for too often having been uncertain, fearful, disheartened, and stumbling, and for often not recognizing God's guidance and not trusting in God's promises. We are painfully aware of all this ourselves. But this does not alter the fact that we as the churches of the Federation were neither

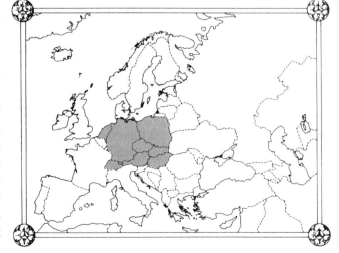

lured onto that road by the spirit of error nor did we embark upon it out of anxiety; rather, it was clearly God's way with us.

God made us sensitive to the problems of human survival and taught us that hope for the shalom of God's kingdom makes it necessary and possible for us to contribute toward maintaining peace, achieving justice, and preserving the creation.

The intensive participation of our Federation in ecumenical work not only helped us to make some headway on the long road towards the visible unity of the churches, but at the same time it made us recognize that the message of God's shalom is God's affirmation of life in this world. The final objective of God's action is not the unified Church but God's Kingdom. This makes the churches responsible to counteract the acute threats to life in this world emanating from injustice, war, and the destruction of nature.

Educating for peace

Clearly the topic of peace claimed our greatest attention. This doubtless was related to the fact that we found ourselves at the dividing line of two antagonistic social systems and two opposing military blocs, and that we witnessed the gigantic stockpiling of military weapons in our country. The suspicion occasionally voiced that the Protestant churches had taken up the issue of peace so vehemently in order to accommodate the state (which had repeatedly asserted that securing peace was a primary objective of its policies) is nonsense. Even if our churches did not question that the state was committed to peace, and even if the chairman of the GDR State Council in his talks with representatives of the Federation of Protestant Churches on March 6, 1978, commended their commitment to peace and international understanding, the churches themselves were never ready to play the role of endorsing the state's foreign policy. No other institution set its own agenda as clearly. Let me name a few examples:

1. When shortly after the talks of March 6, 1978, the churches heard that mandatory paramilitary instruction was to be introduced in the upper school grades, the Conference of Church Leaders immediately and repeatedly let the government know of their grave reservations to this project. Though the churches did not call for a boycott of the instruction they installed an ad hoc committee to work out a basic concept for an "education for peace." Peace education was the church's answer to the state's training in thinking in friend-enemy paradigms, and in taking pleasure in the military.

2. During the Ten Days for Peace in 1981 the security police responded repressively to people wearing badges with the slogan "swords into plowshares." The churches were criticized for allowing groups that demanded the unilateral disarmament of the GDR to gather under their protection. The Conference of Church Leaders undertook difficult talks with the government, in which they defended the slogan as indispensable and defended those who wore the badges, although without much publicity. There is a straight path leading directly from the annual Ten Days for Peace events, prepared by the church youth commission with active youth participation and sponsored by the Conference of Church Leaders, to the events of autumn 1989.

3. During the 1980s the system of military security through deterrence with weapons of mass annihilation became the dominant theme of the churches' peace work. Since the 1982 Federal Synod they continuously demanded reductions of military forces with the objective of supplanting the prevailing military security system with a political one. The 1982 Synod appropriated the concept of "common security" and declared its practical political application one of the prime tasks of the 1980s. Simultaneously, the churches supported all endeavors for political alternatives to supplant the concept of military deterrence. Taking this position, the Synod was ahead of a development that began to be publicly discussed in the GDR only after 1984, and even then the term "equal security" was used instead of "common security." The 1982 Synod had already said that "a clear renunciation of the spirit and logic of deterrence was unavoidable." Later, in 1984, the Federal Synod formally "renounced the spirit, logic, and practice of deterrence." The term "renunciation" was clearly used in its theological sense. This renunciation was expressly repeated in the Peace Confession of the 1987 Federal Synod as being "in obedience to the triune God."

Although the Evangelical Church in Germany (EKD, formerly West German) was not ready to make such a clear statement, we did have the general direction of our peace work in common with the EKD. A Consultative Group formed in 1980 from representatives of the EKD and the Federation of Protestant Churches prepared a working report in 1982, which in itself was a noteworthy expression of our churches' "special fellowship." Although there was not enough common ground for a joint renunciation of deterrence, the report stated: "Our churches must make people aware of the developments in the deterrence system which increasingly endanger peace." Moreover, it says that there are no values whatsoever that would permit the use of nuclear weapons. And the 1985 Joint Declaration on Peace expresses this even more clearly: "Together we are convinced that the system of nuclear deterrence is no permanent way to secure peace. Rather, it must be overcome."

Our No to the deterrence system, of course, had and still has consequences for the issue of military service. The synods repeatedly protested the use of noncombatant construction brigades in military installations. Ever since the early 1980s, the synods continually demanded the institution of an alternative civilian Social Service for Peace, and the synods supported conscientious objectors. In the Peace Confession of 1987 the Federal Synod clearly states: "Every Christian who is faced with having to serve in the military must thoroughly examine whether his decision is in harmony with the gospel of peace. The Christian decision against armed or unarmed military service reflects an obedience of faith which leads into the path of peace." Let us hope that after the Federation is dissolved, its member churches will always remember that in their responsibility for peace they made these statements in obedience to the triune God. Let us hope they will not some day turn over their peace responsibilities

Berlin, the day after the wall fell

Robert C. Lodwick

to special groups out of courtesy or fear that they might be viewed as troublemakers from the East.

Struggling to be faithful

God challenged us in the social context God gave us to walk the narrow path between opposition and opportunism, between complete rejection and complete accommodation, in critical solidarity and mature responsibility.

We have come to the end of that path. The society in which we walked it no longer exists. When the churches in the GDR formed the Federation of Protestant Churches, they did not start from zero but had already lived in the GDR for twenty years and had gathered experience in and with it. Of course, this experience was partially formed by our belonging to a church still officially undivided and by the effect that the Cold War and the Hallstein Doctrine (West Germany's claim to exclusively represent all Germany) had on the relations between church and state.

Two statements from the time just before the Berlin Wall was erected may illustrate the churches' thoughts about the life of the churches and Christians in the GDR. The handout of the United Evangelical Lutheran Church of November 3, 1960, "The Christian in the GDR," says:

The real problem must be seen in the fact that in the GDR the atheistic philosophy is, in a dictatorial and all-encompassing way, the fundamental principle of the state . . . Christians are not only expected to tolerate this condition . . . They are unhappy because they are urged to officially propagate atheism . . . The longer this situation exists the more acute the question becomes whether Christians can still live in the GDR at all. Christians do their duty, but they can only accept and suffer with the fact that they have to live in an atheistic and philosophically materialistic state . . .

Christians hesitate to take an active part in political and social life beyond what duty requires.

The message of the Evangelical Church of the Union of November 1960 to the congregations of its members churches in the GDR was different:

We thank God that we are under God's dominion in both parts of this divided country. . . . We thank our Lord that he has prepared so many people to stay in the GDR in the places he put them. But we are also worried to see how many have left the GDR or are staying full of resentment. We know the urgent reasons to leave and we take them so seriously that we have addressed ourselves to the government of the GDR. We remind our congregations: The Lord says, "Be not afraid!" . . . In the GDR, as everywhere else, all people, powerful and powerless, are in the hands of the Resurrected Lord.

Christians in all walks of life were encouraged to stay in the country. Production workers, for example, were challenged, "See if you can really live to God's honor and the benefit of fellow people in your cooperatives and factories." This was certainly good advice. But only the churches in the GDR themselves could and had to try to find guidance for how we were to live by placing our observations and experience in the light of God's Word. I do not know whether there are many churches who thought so continuously and intensively about their path as we did in the Federation.

Our churches shared in the life and developments of this society, exercised solidarity, criticized and made public statements. This was done in the Sunday services of the congregations and in a more pronounced manner at the meetings of the synod, where the reports of the church leadership were presented to the public and were openly discussed in the presence of state representatives and the press. They commended positive approaches and decisions (such as social policies or modest improvements in travel and visitation policies), not to curry favor with the state nor to avoid always making negative statements, but to encourage the state to move in the right direction. Things that made our society sick and hard to live in were also named on such occasions. I think that nearly all problems of the GDR society were thus broached and damaging developments were analyzed.

Doubtless, in all our talking we overestimated the ability of our state counterparts to listen attentively, to arrive at insights and to change. In some cases we had illusions about their moral integrity; we were not ready to see that for them nothing else counted but the preservation of their power. On the other hand we knew that a wider public was needed than that of a synod if our questions and requests were really to be heard. Some reproached us, believing that we thought it sufficient simply to spell out the shortcomings of the GDR, to address the unpleasant developments that made so many people despair, and to declare that remedies and transformations were necessary. Should we have called for protest actions? It was certainly sobering to see the unwillingness of our church members to resist when it came to the issue of state youth dedications and paramilitary instruction in schools. Still, in spite of all our shortcomings we should ask who spoke more clearly and openly than the Protestant churches? In an interview, Klaus Gysi, former GDR state secretary for church affairs, conceded that in his eyes the Protestant churches not only fought for their own people but for others as well.

Less than prophetic

Let me now state what I believe to be the issues about which we said nothing or too little:

We said nothing official when the wall was erected nor did we join others in the slogan "Down with the wall!" On the other hand, we never used the lie of the "anti-fascist protection wall," and we did talk about the consequences of the wall on the people and demanded steps to alleviate the grave effects.

We said little or nothing about GDR laws and the penal system, although, for example, the Federation expressed reservations and doubts on some sections of the third amendment to the penal code to the government.

We said too little, at least in public, about the activities of the state security service (Stasi), the extent and devilish methods of which have come to light only recently. At least we did warn people in our sermons not to permit themselves to be recruited as informers or to pass on information about others, because doing so would do irreparable harm to the informers themselves.

Of course, we knew that our telephones were bugged and that our mail was being read, that our sermons were being listened to, and that our conversations and meetings were being monitored by Stasi agents. We also had to be aware of the possibility that paid agents were placed in our offices, in leading institutions, and on the boards of the congregations. Often we knew their names. But we refused to be intimidated by distrust and to have our fellowship wrecked.

We also said relatively little about the GDR economy, though we pointed out that a centralized planning system and the policies pursued in education and staffing did harm to the creative capacities of the people. Still, we agreed with the Program on the Unity of Economic and Social Policies, and only recognized and expressed relatively late (although soon enough) how precarious the economic basis of the "social achievements" was, and that the price subsidy system had reached its limit and a more market-oriented price system was needed. But we did not perceive the real condition of our economy, and perhaps we did not want to see it.

It is now evident that we were wrong to think that the socialist system could reform itself. We were ready to take the original intentions of socialism seriously, and to help the people fight their political and social alienation and to exercise their rights. What was called socialism and practiced as such in the GDR has now compromised the word so much that for a long time to come it will be unusable, at least here. As churches we have no reason to join the self-righteous triumphal chorus over the fall of socialism. Rather, we have every reason to turn anew to the biblical message of God's liberating justice, from which socialism got its original inspiration, and thus to continue to help the impoverished, the debased, and the powerless to their rightful human fulfillment.

From talk to action

The Wende (or "turning point," as the 1989 uprising in the GDR was called) was preceded by a long process of consciousness raising and will formation. This would not have happened without the groups that in the early 1980s began to gather in the churches. They were the first to take the decisive steps from meditation and discussion to action and provocation. We did some thorough thinking at the Federation about these groups and their role in the churches. The relations between them and the church leadership were often laden with tensions. The church leadership cautioned them against street demonstrations or spectacular actions. The leadership wanted to ease tension with the state, and the groups wanted to provoke it. They were not ready to accept any advice of

the church leadership on their plans and actions, but at the same time they expected church leaders' support. The church leadership never abandoned anyone. The relationship between church leadership and groups will remain a particularly interesting field of exploration, unless the groups leave the churches, either because they no longer need church space or because the congregations no longer tolerate them. In that case, the churches would lose an essential element of disturbance and movement.

A last word on the question of guilt. Last year much was said about guilty behavior, even that of the churches. Bishops and synods confessed their fearful silence, their shying away from dispute and their entanglement with the system as guilt which was all good to hear in view of the attempts to self-absolution in this country. Of course only rarely was our guilt before God mentioned, our pettiness of faith, our inadequate trust, our feeble courage to witness our faith. Guilt was attributed to the church leadership.

However, Bishop Johannes Hempel has said, "The question of guilt must be handled with care. Insight into guilt must ripen. Repentance takes time, because we must repent for the right thing. And in this regard it is not a question of honesty but of acknowledging what the mistake really was. There will perhaps be many more things for which we must repent than we can see now. Always we shall have to pray in the words of Psalm 19: 'Clear thou me from hidden faults.'"

We traveled a long distance as the Federation of Protestant Churches in the GDR. The journey formed us. So many things happened to us, among us, by us. It is impossible to collect it all in a speech like this, or ever collect it at all. Even if the things we accomplished may be small, I would like to remind us of the words from the great chapter of Jesus' resurrection in the New Testament: "Be steadfast, immovable, always excelling in the work of the Lord, because you know that in the Lord your labor is not in vain." (1 Cor. 15:58) Nothing is in vain! If all things must serve those who love God, so also must these things.

Now we must also look ahead. What was said at the Federation's 1973 Synod in Schwerin about our journey into the reality of the GDR can also be applied to the things ahead of us: "Jesus Christ will walk before us into the new social situation and he will prepare it for us as a field of mission and as a chance to serve."

Werner Krusche is bishop emeritus of Magdeburg, Germany.

Afterword: Unification Brings New Problems

Barbara Green

The Berlin Wall was breached on November 9, 1989, the 51st anniversary of Kristallnacht (Crystal Night), a single night in which Nazis destroyed Jewish businesses and synagogues throughout Germany. As early as January 1990, with the political future of East Germany far from certain, church leaders from the East and West began preliminary talks toward unifying the churches. An interim government was elected in East Germany, which negotiated a treaty of unification with West Germany throughout the summer of 1990. East German currency was replaced by West German currency on July 1, 1990. Formal unification took place on October 3, 1990, since then a national holiday.

The East German Federation of Protestant Churches was dissolved in February 1991 and the unification of the Evangelical Church in Germany, East and West, took place later that spring.

Yet that ceremony marked only the beginning of the problems of unification. Churches in the two regions still faced radical differences in the social contexts for their ministries. East Germans faced massive unemployment as inefficient enterprises were closed down, and lived in relative poverty in the midst of West German overabundance. Although most disdained the old East German state, they found that its dissolution brought them a deeper crisis of national identity than they could have expected. West Germans, on the other hand, faced heavy tax increases to finance needs in the East and possible threats to their jobs from an influx of cheaper labor, as well as an end to the complacency of their own national identity.

Even now, the wall in people's heads is still standing. Peter Beier, moderator of the West German Synod of the Rhineland, noted in a July 1994 address to the Evangelical Church of the Union, "The difference between people from the West and people from the East is nowhere near overcome. Forty years of separated church history have kept us from growing together seamlessly."

A further complication to the context has been the massive inflow of refugees from the Yugoslav wars, gypsies, asylum seekers from Africa, Asia, and the Middle East, ethnic Germans from Russia and Romania, and even a few Jews from Russia. Social services are strained to provide for them and every community is impacted by new arrivals. In 1993 immigration laws were made more restrictive, with only token opposition from the churches. Harassment of foreigners by neo-nazi groups and riots in some cities have resulted in fatalities in several communities in both East and West. In 1993 a visitation group from the World Council of Churches urged the German churches to establish a Program to Combat Racism in Germany, and the German churches have begun to implement the suggestion.

What to do with the history—and the files—of the East German secret police, the Stasi, has been particularly troublesome. Federal law now permits individual victims of Stasi spying to review their own files, which remain restricted from everyone else. But collaborators' files and institutional files are available to the press, and western journalists have published books of this material, often with commentaries intended to undermine the credibility of East German church leaders. Each regional synod in the former East has made its own decision on whether to have every church employee's records searched for possible evidence of collaboration. Some sensational cases of collaboration have emerged, causing particular pain among parishioners.

> Some sensational cases of collaboration have emerged, causing particular pain among parishioners.

The three issues dogging the unification process for the churches have been church finances, religious instruction, and military chaplaincy. The West German churches are financed by a church tax system collected by the government together with regular income tax. The East German churches were financed by a system of voluntary contributions, supplemented by hard currency contributions from the

West. Now the church tax system has been implemented in the East, and combined with the high rates of unemployment, has in many cases resulted in a net loss of income to the churches.

West German public schools provide for religious instruction in the schools. This was forbidden in the East and afterschool "Sunday School-style" classes were held in the churches. Now that system has been disbanded, but what to teach in its place to atheism-hardened young people is an ongoing dilemma in the public schools in the East, as is the question of who should teach these classes.

The West German churches had a contract with the West German military to provide chaplains under military discipline. East Germans used local pastors near base sites to minister to young conscripts. They objected to state control over clergy implied in the West German system. A new unified system of ministry to the military is still being negotiated, and its contours are controversial. The World Council of Churches' program for Justice, Peace, and the Integrity of Creation (JPIC) played a key role in East Germany in preparing the 1989 revolution. A series of three JPIC assemblies was held there in the late 1980s, and became a popular forum for articulating grievances against the regime. After 1989 the process collapsed, as people were overwhelmed by their new circumstances. Now the Ecumenical Council of Berlin has called for reviving the JPIC process. It has sketched out a platform to include: a civilian peace service alternative to military conscription specializing in nonviolent

Presbyterian Record/John Congram

Matthias Church in Budapest, Hungary

conflict resolution, a campaign to limit German arms exports, a campaign to find a civilian alternative to "full military honors" for visiting heads of state, efforts to reverse the growth in community violence, especially among young people, strengthening peace education in the schools, and a campaign against violence in the media. An ecumenical assembly met in Dresden the first Sunday of Advent 1994 to continue the JPIC work.

The Kirchentag (church day) movement is another arena where churches are working to bridge the gap between church and society. It arose in post-World War II Germany to provide adult lay education, so that ignorance could never again permit German laity to become complicit in evil. In recent years the biennial five-day event has become a mammoth diverse social forum, taxing the resources of major cities. 125,000 people attended the 1993 Kirchentag in Munich, sixty-one percent of whom were younger than thirty years of age. The 1995 Kirchentag will be held in Hamburg, and the 1997 one is planned for Leipzig. The motto for the Hamburg event comes from Micah 6: "You know what the Lord requires of you."

The Kirchentag movement intends to answer the loss of orientation, identity and conviction in post-Cold War, postmodern Germany. That ancient admonition "to do justice, love mercy, and walk humbly with your God" will guide the German churches through an uncertain future.

Barbara Green is Associate in the Washington Office of the Presbyterian Church (USA). From 1977 to 1981 she was liaison from the National Council of Churches in the USA to the Federation of Protestant Churches in East Germany.

Zoltan Bona, general secretary of the Ecumenical Council of Hungary

Church Life in Hungary

Reliable religious statistics have not been available in Hungary since 1948, but it is generally accepted that the population is nominally sixty percent Catholic, twenty percent Reformed, and ten percent Lutheran. The percentage of active believers is probably much lower: At most, sixty percent of Hungarians call themselves Christian. There is mutual respect among the denominations and, with the exception of the Catholics, they all belong to the Hungarian Ecumenical Council and all, including the Catholics, are involved in joint worship and other ecumenical activities.

During communist times many church people, clerical and lay, made their accommodation with the regime in a variety of ways, by supporting the regime's programs such as "peace priests" or "diakonia," or even by collaborating with open or secret organs of government. Memories of what Reformed Bishop Lorand Hegedus called "the qualitative differences in people's conduct" color and influence people's estimates of themselves and each other, creating an atmosphere of suspicion and distrust. Reconciliation is an even greater problem in the churches than in everyday life.

One of the biggest tasks facing the Hungarian churches in the aftermath of communism is that of rebuilding and renewing the spiritual life of their members. Lutheran Bishop Bela Harmati spoke of arriving in a provincial town to carry out a baptism of five children. On enquiring, he found that none of the parents or godparents had been baptized either, so he finished by baptizing thirty-eight souls. There is great hunger for religion, said Bishop Harmati, but not necessarily for that provided by the traditional churches. Anyone can go around preaching and register a church with his followers, so there is a great need to educate people in what the traditional Lutheran and Reformed churches stand for.

—*CAREE Communicator*, Fall 1994

5 Minutes to 3

In many villages of southern Hungary, the congregations of the Reformed Churches were usually too poor to have a real clock on their church tower. When I participated in the rededication of the church in the village of Old and then visited other villages, I noticed that these painted clocks all had the hands painted at five minutes to three. I thought to myself that at least the clocks were accurate twice a day!

Then I discovered that the people had chosen this time as symbolic of their faith, for Christ was crucified at the third hour. Therefore, they still had five minutes to repent of their sins. The Communist authorities never painted over these clocks. Did they not understand the symbolism? If they didn't, the elderly villagers did and shared the story with their children and grandchildren as a constant reminder to remain faithful to their Christian faith.

—*Robert C. Lodwick*

Village church at Old, Hungary

The Church Throughout Changes in Czechoslovakia

Jakub Trojan

In February 1948, the Communist Party assumed power in Czechoslovakia following a cabinet crisis which lasted several days. Immediately it enforced a number of political and social measures that began to change the social system from its very foundations. Radical changes were made in all areas of ownership. Initially this concerned industry, trade, and banking, and after the beginning of the 1950s to an ever increasing degree, agriculture. With the passage of the new constitution of Czechoslovakia in 1960, the country was declared a socialist republic allied to the Soviet Union.

However, unlike the other satellites in the Soviet bloc (East Germany, Poland, Hungary, Romania, and Bulgaria), socialism did not gain the upper hand in Czechoslovakia by mere external force. The idea of social justice and the equality of citizens without conspicuous differences in ownership had been alive in our nation for decades, ever since the end of the nineteenth century. Another contributing factor was a positive bias toward Russia, which was seen as the land of our Slavonic brothers. Even after its adoption of a Bolshevik orientation at the close of the 1920s, the Communist Party of Czechoslovakia held a strong position within the democratic system. During World War II, it was engaged to a significant extent in the resistance government.

The failure of the western powers, Great Britain and France, the closest allies of Czechoslovakia during the period between World War I and World War II and the guarantors of its independence since 1918, was still a vivid and painful memory. At Munich, the British and French had signed a humiliating agreement with Nazi Germany and Fascist Italy which they forced upon Czechoslovakia. It immediately resulted in considerable territorial concessions to Germany (autumn 1938) and shortly thereafter, in the German occupation of Bohemia and Moravia (March 1939). The broad spectrum of postwar Czechoslovakia, restored to its original borders of 1937, adopted a pro-Soviet position quite naturally, for the Soviets were regarded as having defeated the enemy and liberated the land.

From the birth of the modern Czechoslovakia, churches remained more or less on the periphery of social events. Until the beginning of the war in 1939, the majority Catholic church found it difficult to recover from its weakened position incurred by centuries-old cooperation with the Austrian monarchy. After 1918 more than two million Catholics withdrew, either to join the newly founded national Czechoslovak Church, the Evangelical Church of Czech Brethren (ECCB), or to remain without any church affiliation at all, due to a postwar wave of secularization. Enfeebled in its theology and church life, Czech Catholicism began to acquire a new self-confidence initially in the cultural realm and later in a political context during the Munich crisis. During the war it successfully aspired to be the defender of national identity.

Protestant churches in the regions of Bohemia and Moravia had traditionally been in the minority. Even the largest, the Evangelical Church of Czech Brethren, was numerically only a fraction of

Cathedral in Prague

Robert C. Lodwick

what the majority church could claim (Catholics: approximately 8 million, ECCB: 250,000). However, even as a minority, it made a notable impact on the history of the country. Its desire was that the Czech nation become once again the nation of the fifteenth-century reformer Jan Hus, rooted in the truth of Christ, devoted to the Scripture, faithful to its spiritual heritage. From the pulpit and in church publications it conscientiously strove to connect basic biblical motifs with the social problems that had begun to develop dramatically at the close of the 1920s, during the Depression, and after Hitler's accession to power in neighboring Germany. But despite these and other similar efforts, it remained on the margin.

Other churches fared no better. In general, Christianity in Czechoslovakia offered no program to address all areas of life, both personal and societal. There was an obvious closed-mindedness and an inability to grasp the most profound questions and problems of the modern world as it was becoming increasingly secularized. Ideas that could have borne any weight were lacking. What prevailed was manifested in Catholicism by empty ceremonies and in Protestantism by a gradual escape into congregational seclusion with a judgmental attitude toward the world.

Not even in the decisive period from 1945 to 1948 did the churches stand in the forefront of the struggle for a new spiritual and moral obligation, to present the public with a well-thought-out conception for solving burning domestic and international problems. At best, when they did venture out beyond the walls of their churches and cathedrals, they pled for tolerance and loyal discipline, and encouraged people to orient themselves around fundamental values. In principle, however, the churches were unprepared for the enormous changes that postwar developments brought to all aspects of life. Let it be repeated: We are talking about changes that had deep domestic roots and were not forced upon us from the outside alone.

The churches were also unprepared for the fundamental turning point in February 1948. From the outset, it was obvious that the changes that were to take place would inevitably have a profound effect on religion and the life of the churches, and indeed, they swiftly ensued. As early as October 1949, under Communist pressure, the highest legislative body enacted laws that were to govern state policy regarding the church for what turned out to be forty long years. Without allowing the churches to present their own views on the subject, the state proclaimed its decision to assume the burden of paying the salaries of all the clergy in all the churches. Of course, prior to this, all church property had been nationalized. The Catholic Church was most affected since it was one of the largest landowners. Another provision of this legislation gave the state the sole right to grant permission to perform church service and ministry on all levels, significantly limiting the free choice or appointment of clergy according to internal church order. This forced the churches into dependency on a state bureaucracy that was essentially run by the party apparatus and security agents of the Ministry of Interior, all in harmony with militantly atheistic propaganda.

After seizing power and liquidating their political opponents in other parties, the major concern of the Communists became the disposition of the potentially dangerous opposition on the side of what they were convinced was a threat—the Catholic Church. The principal aim of the Communists was to isolate the Catholic hierarchy from the masses of believers. The government adopted the tactical maneuver of pretending that the attack on leading representatives of the Catholic Church was not an attack on religion as such nor by any means on the church itself.

Protestants were even allowed to establish new congregations during the 1950s, arousing the false hope that they were to be counted upon to morally and spiritually nurture society. The same strategy was employed to win over the lower ranking Catholic clergy and their ordinary parish members.

A concentrated attack was directed against the Vatican. People within the church found themselves under the pressure of the authorities who alleged

> What prevailed was...
> a gradual escape into
> congregational seclusion with
> a judgmental attitude
> toward the world.

they were submissive instruments of Rome. Methods in this conflict ranged from administrative manipulation to outright violence on the part of the state. Monastic orders were dissolved. Their members were sent away to prison or military work camps for years, along with others who for one reason or another were undesirable to the regime.

And so after a few years, ruling forces succeeded in "pacifying" the society. Leftist-oriented strata actively and enthusiastically participated out of conviction in building a new social order, while others passively adapted themselves in the end.

The first shock to deeply penetrate the society ruled by the Communist Party came in the last half of the 1950s, when Nikita Khrushchev revealed Stalinist crimes at the 20th Party Congress in the USSR. The first wave of criticism to raise fundamental questions of morals, culture, and politics swept through the country, with the participation of writers, journalists, and intellectuals within and without the party.

For the first time voices were heard demanding more respect for domestic democratic and spiritual traditions. There was an isolated appeal of the churches calling for a moral and spiritual renewal because—as was stated in a memorandum to the cabinet conceived by the Czech Protestant theologian, Josef L. Hromádka, and his colleagues—the entire society had found itself in the midst of a deep crisis.

At that time, however, the regime was still strong enough to swiftly initiate a counter-offensive. The leading strategy was to keep the church from interfering with problems of society. Religion was proclaimed a private affair. No official documents recorded church membership. Atheistic propaganda increased. The only officially acceptable view became Marxism-Leninism, and subscribing to it became a prerequisite for anyone who sought a position in the field of education.

This struck a sensitive chord for Czech Protestants in particular, who had highly prized education for centuries. In Protestant circles, the teaching profession was among one of the favorite career choices young people made. The same was true for the medical professions—in other words, for the humanitarian sciences in general. So when the regime laid down ideological barriers to entrance into universities, especially in the pedagogical field, and accepted only those who professed the officially proclaimed ideology, that meant the young people were forced either to accommodate the demand or to abandon all hope of a future in the field of education.

Josef Lukl Hromádka

Born in Moravia in 1889, Josef Hromádka was a leading Czech theologian, ecumenist and pioneer of Christian-Marxist dialogue, founder of the Christian Peace Conference, vice-president of the World Alliance of Reformed Churches, Professor at Princeton Theological Seminary and, returning to Prague, Dean of the Comenius Faculty of Protestant Theology.

Convinced that "Western civilization" was a spent force in world history, Hromádka emphasized the socialist vision of a society "in which man will be free of all external greed, mammon and material tyranny, and in which a fellowship of real human beings in mutual sympathy, love and goodwill will be established."

When Warsaw pact troops invaded Czechoslovakia in 1968, crushing the "Prague spring" and its effort to build "socialism with a human face," Hromádka wrote to the ambassador of the USSR in Prague that "the Soviet government could not have committed a more tragic error. . . . The moral weight of socialism and communism has been shattered for a long time to come. Only an immediate withdrawal of the occupation forces would, at least in part, moderate our common misfortune."

In a tribute at his funeral in 1970, WCC general secretary Eugene Carson Blake, calling Hromádka "a man of hope . . . despite his deep disappointments," noted that "many Americans during the cold war supposed he must be a communist and therefore an enemy, while many communists distrusted his loyalty even while for 21 years he was the strongest force in Eastern Europe in persuading his fellow churchmen to support in faith and hope their revolutionary socialist governments and societies. During these same 21 years he was the outstanding moral interpreter to the West of the vision of justice and peace that has inspired the best in the socialist nations."

—from the *Dictionary of the Ecumenical Movement* (WCC Publications and Wm B. Eerdmans, 1991)

The result was a blatant violation of human rights. The teaching profession was accessible solely to those who had become members of the only legal youth organization and who were not burdened with "religious prejudices." Of course, this was not the only profession so affected. The practice had a negative impact on the whole society.

Within the framework of the cultural revolution, worship was practically the only activity the regime allowed the church. This applied to such traditional forms of activity as adult Bible study, Sunday School for children, occasional specialized courses involving Christian services, youth, and so on. In small towns in particular, congregations were watched by a network of informers. On county and regional levels, state appointed "church secretaries" controlled pastors who were constantly under threat of having their ministerial licenses revoked. Because all fields of activity throughout society were ruled by one party and its ideology, even the traditional forms of church life had to count on their church members, especially if they were active, being in the disfavor of the authorities. This was first manifested in difficulties their children experienced when they sought entrance into schools, especially at higher levels.

The attempt to humanize socialism began in Czechoslovakia in the early 1960s when the second wave of criticism emerged, opening up all of society to a dialogue into which even Christians were drawn. By that time they had already discussed within the church in the last half of the previous decade the secular interpretation of the gospel and were theologically prepared for an encounter with "the world."

For the first time since 1948, theologians were able to publish in the secular press, and journalists and outstanding personalities in the fields of culture and literature were invited to lecture and join in a discussion of alternative views, as well as of cultural and spiritual problems. Even among the ruling powers a diversification was occurring, which culminated in the January election of Alexander Dubcek as general secretary of the Communist Party. Socialism with a human face became the political doctrine of the day.

Once again the churches became conscious of their irreplaceable function in the life of the nation and society and resolved to bear witness to the most profound sources of pastoral and communal life. They attempted to break down the walls of the ghetto into which they had been pushed by their oppressors, although at times they had sought refuge there themselves when they had chosen to adapt to the situation in an effort to survive. Numbers of Catholic priests and monks who had been forbidden for years to perform their spiritual offices returned to the ministry. A sense of service prevailed among them that surmounted any feeling of injustice, and the will to forgive won out over the desire for revenge.

Before it could bear its irrevocable fruits in all areas of society, the reform movement in Czechoslovakia was crushed in August 1968 by the brutal intervention of the armies of the Soviet Union, Bulgaria, Hungary, Poland, and the German Democratic Republic. The decisive criterion for advancement or termination of one's career became approval or disapproval to the encroachment of the armies of the Warsaw Pact. A new wave of immigration to the West set in. The violent enforcement of adaptation and the repression of freedom of speech meant the death of personal initiative, demoralizing the broad spectrum of the population. In the eyes of the public, socialism lost all its attraction, once and for all.

Churches posed a very specific problem for the new regime of Gustáv Husák, and here the process of "normalization" lasted longest, for the manipulators of party and state organs were unable to penetrate into internal church structures. Small Protestant churches (The Brethren Church, Baptists, Methodists, The Union of Brethren) reacted to the changing situation by retreating back into the old framework to which they had become accustomed before 1968, emphasizing primarily one's innermost spiritual life, repentance of the individual, and moral charity. The situation in the Evangelical Church of the Czech Brethren was more complex, for it had experienced considerable exposure in the spring of 1968 as it had spoken out for reform. In

> The violent enforcement of adaptation and the repression of freedom of speech meant the death of personal initiative...

February 1969, its highest legislative body adopted the "Proclamation of the Synod Addressed to the Nation," in which it defended the fundamental motifs of societal renewal from the position of the gospel as they had been crystallized in the reform efforts.

The authorities began their method of "slicing off salami" on county and regional levels by dealing with figures in key positions. Soon ecumenical cooperation among Christians on a congregational and parish basis was disrupted. The regime permitted it to continue solely at the highest levels, creating an artificially maintained facade of ecumenical relations which it employed to prove its toleration.

From the early 1970s, the regime did everything in its power to push the churches back once again into their cathedrals and meeting houses, forbidding any activity that might influence events in the society. Official rhetoric was void of any mention of the positive contribution of churches in moral training—a fundamental departure from the position proclaimed by the state when the Communists gained power. Christianity as such was regarded as a hostile ideology that had to be eradicated. Middle-aged church members in particular dropped out, because they still wanted to function in society. Unlike the situation during the cultural revolution, this time their departure was not accompanied by having a bad conscience. A secularized way of life, whether expressly atheistic or not, became much more "normal" during this process than it had been in the early 1950s.

Within the Catholic Church there was an attempt to organize an underground church, alongside the heavily destroyed official one, with a strong laity, secretly consecrated priests, and a few bishops. Simultaneously, the regime was cultivating a peace movement of Catholic clergy called Pacem in Terris, naturally condemned by the Vatican, through which it wanted to split the church apart from within.

A similar attempt to divide Protestants was made that even went so far as to employ the secret security apparatus. For example, through the assistance of state church secretaries on county and regional levels a so-called "agency of influence" was created from the ranks of presbyters and pastors, which was to intervene in church institutions, influencing the work of their administration, convents, and synods.

This painful lack of power to resist the repressive regime was manifest in Czechoslovak society outside of the church as well. Every facet of its life was inhibited by administrative manipulation and pressure,

St. Vitus' Church in Prague

affecting institutions, companies and organizations of every sort. The sad reality is that the churches did not demonstrate greater spiritual resistance but let themselves become mutually divided, allowing the social dimension of their witness to be taken away, while all congregational and parish life was essentially limited to acts of liturgy and worship. For the most part this was undoubtedly the result of the continuous pressure of all the factors compiling such a system of oppression. Nevertheless, the internal weakness of the congregation and individual Christians combined to create a climate of submission. Here Christianity in Czechoslovakia stands face to face with a stain it will have to come to terms with for generations to come. The disturbing question is asked: Why did the power of "the world" prove stronger than the spiritual power of the gospel, which was publicly proclaimed and professed in houses of worship?

Charter 77

On January 1, 1977, a group of 242 persons signed a declaration that came to be known as Charter 77. It was a protest document signed by former Communists expelled from the party, democrats, humanists, artists, and members of various churches, including several Catholic priests and eight pastors of the Evangelical Church of the Czech Brethren, plus a large number of Protestant and Catholic laity. Charter 77 soon became more than a document. As it gathered momentum and international publicity, it became a movement even though many of its leaders were imprisoned. Václav Havel was imprisoned three times for supporting human rights through participation in Charter 77.

Charter 77 was created following the publication of a number of pacts and treaties regarding civil, political and cultural rights, which had been incorporated into the laws of our country in the autumn of 1976. By signing the Charter, members expressed their decision to enter into a dialogue with those in power that would lead it to respect in the domestic sphere all the internationally valid legal norms. The difficulty of the situation was intensified because the administration of the country, the very ones who for the most part were responsible for the defiling of the whole society by forcing it into the appalling image of what for years had been called a "naturally" functioning conformity, did not seek dialogue in the slightest. All it was interested in was maintaining its own power, not in solving the crisis.

One could have expected that the churches would adhere to the efforts of Charter 77 for a radical renewal. Instead of a courageous witness and a willingness to support those citizens who had taken the risk of a nonconformist position upon themselves, under state pressure, the voices that could be heard from church headquarters expressed at best bewilderment and at worst dissociation from Charter 77 members. As late as the close of the 1970s, when the activity of the first Chartists began, official documents of churches and of the Comenius Theology Faculty of the ECCB (as well as others) reiterated their opinion that socialism was to be considered a framework within which we as Christians could carry out our work.

The work of Charter 77 continued despite the fact that it was isolated and received support from the society only in secret and most often from individuals. Gradually it put out through *samizdat* (the Russian word denoting the clandestine system for circulating mimeographed documents denied official publication) a series of documents in which it adopted positions on various social problems. This stimulated within the heretofore silent and silenced society a discussion concerning questions that official propaganda either played down or passed over. Soon after the original Charta document came out, rather intensive discussions began, initially within the movement itself, where it was not exceptional for theologians to be invited to lecture in surroundings where they would hardly have gone before.

Such encounters transversed all confessional barriers. Shortly after that, a vast range of groups and seminars began to work together regularly on social, economic, and political issues. Philosophical and theological seminars took shape, and *samizdat* material of all kinds was "published." Home theaters as well as unofficial art exhibits were organized. A second culture was born.

And what about the churches? How did they become involved in the process of intellectual preparation for fundamental changes in society? The answer is not simple. Catholics chose the way of seeking a new spirituality. As I have already mentioned, a secret community of believers was formed, led by active lay people and priests whom they trusted. There was a strong emphasis placed on spiritual nurturing within the family, and Catholic *samizdat* literature of a theological, philosophical, and general nature was of relatively high quality. Home seminars were operative where ecumenical discussions between Catholics and Protestants took place. In 1987, a well-thought-out project of ten-year renewal appeared, which was intended as the foundation for ecumenical cooperation to which Protestants were invited.

During this period within Protestant churches, and especially the ECCB, there was obvious internal tension. A few other pastors signed the Charta, raising the number to about seven percent of the 250 ministers within the church. The New Orientation, which comprised the largest number of Chartists (ministers and laity), became influential for the younger generation within the church, a fact that made the secret security police quite nervous, according to their records. On the other hand, approximately ten percent of the clergy are believed to have cooperated with the secret police, representing only a slightly smaller amount than those in the

> **Official church documents reiterated that socialism was to be considered a framework within which we as Christians could carry out our work.**

Catholic Church.

The November revolution of 1989 found the church in an ambivalent situation. A smaller portion of its members, lay and clergy, had been involved for some time in dissident movements, while the majority had decided to wait it out and avoid conflicts with the powers that be, whose interference into church life never diminished, even up to the very end of their control. As late as 1988, they threatened to revoke the state licenses of several ECCB ministers. State church secretaries in collaboration with the secret police and the "agency of influence" within the church attempted to push through the interests of the regime by, for example, preventing the election of certain people to church office. Still operating were such institutions as the tamely accommodating Christian Peace Conference, designed for export, and the Pacem in Terris, to the increasing indignation of Catholics. The Ecumenical Council of Churches was also still under pressure, to which it conformed. All of these institutions were used by the regime to divide the church from within, as well as for influencing foreign ecclesiastical bodies abroad.

Revolution begins

The dramatic events of the ten days beginning with November 17, 1989, when special forces brutally attacked a peaceful and officially approved student demonstration, until the successful general strike of November 27, flung even the leadership of individual churches into action. Cardinal Tomásek publicly proclaimed his solidarity with the formation of the Civic Forum in which Václav Havel played a leading role.

The 26th Synod of the Evangelical Church of the Czech Brethren was in session just at the time when the revolution began. It readily reacted to the emergent situation and commissioned the Synodal Senior, Dr. Josef Hromádka, student of but unrelated to Professor Josef L. Hromádka mentioned earlier, to protest directly to the Premier against the brutal police attack and to discuss with him any further measures. In the days that followed, the Senior himself became a deputy premier in the cabinet. After ten days in which the nation's history swiftly strode through enormous revolutionary changes every few minutes, it became clear that our society had taken its earlier "time out" so that in the end it could successfully culminate those previous attempts at reform that had come to nothing, due to brutal interference from either within or without.

Sculpture in Prague commemorating students beaten or killed by police

It is remarkable that the gatherings of hundreds of thousands of people, including a large percentage of young people, on Wenceslaus Square beginning on November 20, or at Letna on November 25 and 26, had more than a merely political character. They manifested to an increasing extent a moral and spiritual dimension and even displayed an almost religious ritual. Often the "Prayer for Martha," a favorite song dating back to the time of the Prague Spring, was sung. It expresses the deep conviction that "after the storm has passed, the rule of your own affairs will be returned to you, O people"—an incomplete fragment taken from the "Testament of the Dying Mother of Unitas Fratrum," written by John Amos Comenius, the famous seventeenth-century leader of the Czech Reformation, a pedagogue, thinker, and politician. Here in a pop music tune was concentrated the desire of the nation as expressed by the last bishop of the Brethren Union!

There were words of confession uttered at the demonstration by leading dissidents, and Václav Havel in particular, that we had conformed for years to a regime that had trampled over our dignity. As citizens we had lacked courage and thus prolonged the rule of darkness by our own volition. For years we had not believed that things could be changed. Instead of rising up to civic responsibility, we had been subservient. This was a public profession of our sins! On November 23, when the foremost figure of the events of 1968, Alexander Dubcek, spoke to the people of Prague, many realized that they were witnessing a great moment of rehabilitation for those who had not forsaken their convictions even at the price of great tribulation. During such moments participants of the demonstrations experienced a moral cleansing. United in guilt from the past and yet in the hope that the end of slavery was at hand, we stood in the streets and squares staggered by the miracle of freedom we had been given.

Perhaps I can dare to make the claim that this manifestation of civic resolve, extending beyond the means of routine politics or practices of revolt, was to a certain extent a co-creation of the witness of nonconforming Christians as well as of those who continued to work in official churches, clergy and laity alike. It was a special moment for all who carried out their tasks faithfully, not dissociating themselves from those who had entered into open conflict with the regime. Many of us who had chosen the path of nonconformity experienced the power of intercessory prayer as well as practical assistance during the years we were forcefully separated from work in the church. A group of ECCB pastors who had been among the first to sign the Charter had tried to express this in a statement sent out in January 1977: "All those who conscientiously prepare their sermons, faithfully provide pastoral care, and seek out the ill, elderly, and desolate stand together in one and the same struggle with us in the Charta movement who are standing up for human rights."

At this point I would like to recall the important words of the apostle in I Peter 5:9, that tell us that brothers and sisters the world over are united by the same measure of suffering. One does not have to undergo the same risk or bear the same distress, but can be united with others, despite all situational differences, by the same measure of suffering. During times of discrimination whenever we stood undivided in solidarity, totalitarian power collided with a wall with which it could not cope. At such times we had a foretaste of the future victory which was finally given to us during the November revolution.

In the first few weeks after the revolution the church was faced with a serious problem: everybody adapted to the new situation quickly and with undisguised facility. The walls of the ghetto into which the church had allowed itself to be pushed by the former regime tumbled down under the vociferous shouts of those who rushed without thinking into political activity in newly emerging parties and movements for national and societal renewal. Former dissidents suddenly found themselves in opposition to those who were entering the political arena without sensing the contradiction between what they were doing and how they had acted only a short time before. They had not faced the overwhelming question of coming to terms with their own past where they had expressed more contempt for civic involvement than understanding.

The aversion in the churches against coming to terms with the past is related to the phenomena which appeared in the first months after the revolution. Not just Christianity as a whole, but the churches as such were given credit for the mere fact that they had experienced the ill favor of the former regime for decades. A well-wishing attitude toward the churches was prevalent among the public, to which they responded—especially the Catholics—with a certain sense of triumphalism. One could hear the churches' leadership proclaiming the time had come for the great rehabilitation of Christianity. The spiritual vacuum created after the liquidation of Marxism-Leninism as the official doctrine had to be filled.

It is startling that in the delightful breeze of this historical rehabilitation the difference between sustaining and misleading traditions was forgotten. By no means can we succumb to the illusion that it is possible to transplant the Christian message into Czech society, which has been spiritually and morally devastated, without critical self-searching. The spirit of triumphalism has so obscured the minds of some church leaders that they have taken up the struggle to win the souls of secularized men and women without having repented themselves. At this point as well we find ourselves in the midst of an exacting discussion with the majority of the church, which refuses to face up to the past and lacks the courage to take notice of its guilt.

The church is faced with new tasks in these changing circumstances. We have to accept the

> United in guilt from the past and yet in the hope that the end of slavery was at hand, we stood in the streets and squares staggered by the miracle of freedom we had been given.

46

gospel anew with its universal message that touches all spheres of life, public and private. We cannot tolerate such reduction of that message, as we did in the past, to include only the inner life of the soul and the narrow community of the congregation or parish. The universality of the gospel commits us to global responsibility.

Christians in central and eastern Europe must not relinquish responsibility for the modification of the social system now being constituted following the fall of communism. In all the varieties of its implementation a market economy must possess a character of service, never becoming an end unto itself. It needs just as much alert critical observation as any other system. Based on biblical presuppositions, we must strive to bring into its structures the motifs of cooperation, partnership, and mutuality, and to emphasize the deeper sources of life. None of these is an integral part of it. We have to work toward these goals not only at home but also in the international context. The weaker members of our planetary community need our help as badly as those who are shoved into the margins of our own society.

Truth and tolerance

Churches have to understand the soul of the secularized person, who must never become the mere passive object of their mission and evangelical activity. He or she is also raising questions and presenting his or her own self-understanding, which proves that we are all standing in an open cosmos, where no one has definitive answers. He or she must become to us what we must be to them: partners on the woeful path of history, where we are traveling with the hope that the groaning of all creation (Romans 8) will not fling us back into nothingness but toward new beginnings and the final victory.

Czech Christianity must see to it that Europe as a continent of countless traditions examines them down to the most intrinsic roots, studies them patiently and then illuminates those that overcome egocentricity and demonstrate an inspirational strength necessary for meeting the tasks surfacing before humanity today. It is also essential that we contribute to the birth of a planetary community for whose creation Europe must strive with the same enthusiasm that it displays in the construction of its own house. Here there is a role to be played not only by the largest nations of Europe. All of us are called to bring a specific contribution to the creation of a Europe that will

© Wolf Kutnahorsky/WCC

Pastor Pivonka, Evangelical Church of the Czech Brethren, visiting prisoners in Prague

not be a threat but a partner to the other continents. For Czech and Slovak Christians the renewal of Europe must be an outgrowth of the requirements for renewal, truth and tolerance of our own best traditions. Of course, this selective, difficult intellectual work is no less demanding than monastic discipline, and the results will not be evident for decades. A deep anchorage in the Truth is essential.

Let us remember these words of Jesus: "For this I was born, and for this I came into the world, to testify to the truth." (John 18:37). Here lies the source of our strength and never-ending hope.

Jakub Trojan, member of the Church of the Czech Brethren, is dean and professor of systematic theology at the Protestant Theological School of Charles University in Prague, Czech Republic. From 1974 to 1990, he was deprived of the permission to be a pastor by the Czechoslovak government and was one of the original signers of Charter 77. An expanded version of this article was published in Religion in Eastern Europe, *Vol. XIV, No. 1, February 1994.*

In Our Postmodern Age, a Search for Self-Transcendence

Václav Havel

There are good reasons for suggesting that the modern age has ended. Many things indicate that we are going through a transitional period, when it seems that something is on the way out and something else is painfully being born. It is as if something were crumbling, decaying and exhausting itself, while something else, still indistinct, arises from the rubble.

The distinguishing features of transitional periods are a mixing and blending of cultures and a plurality or parallelism of intellectual and spiritual worlds. These are periods when all consistent value systems collapse, when cultures distant in time and space are discovered or rediscovered. New meaning is gradually born from the encounter, or the intersection, of many different elements.

Today, this state of mind, or of the human world, is called postmodernism. For me, a symbol of that state is a Bedouin mounted on a camel and clad in traditional robes under which he is wearing jeans, with a transistor radio in his hands and an ad for Coca-Cola on the camel's back. I am not ridiculing this, nor am I shedding an intellectual tear over the commercial expansion of the West that destroys alien cultures. I see it as a typical expression of this multicultural era, a signal that an amalgamation of cultures is taking place. I see it as proof that something is being born, that we are in a phase when one age is succeeding another, when everything is possible . . . .

We live in the postmodern world, where everything is possible and almost nothing is certain. This state of affairs has its social and political consequences. The planetary system to which we all belong confronts us with global challenges. We stand helpless before them because our civilization has essentially globalized only the surface of our lives.

But our inner selves continue to have a life of their own. And the fewer answers the era of rational knowledge provides to the basic questions of human being, the more deeply it would seem that people cling to the ancient certainties of their tribe. Because of this, individual cultures, increasingly lumped together by contemporary civilization, are realizing with new urgency their own inner autonomy and the inner differences of other cultures. Cultural conflicts are increasing and are more dangerous today than at any other time in history.

Politicians are rightly worried by the problem of finding the key to ensure the survival of a civilization that is global and multicultural: how respected mechanisms of peaceful coexistence can be set up and on what set of principles they are to be established. These questions have been highlighted with particular urgency by the two most important political events in the second half of the twentieth century, the collapse of colonial hegemony and the fall of communism. The artificial world order of the past decades has collapsed and a new, more just order has not yet emerged.

The central political task of the final years of this century, then, is the creation of a new model of coexistence among the various cultures, peoples, races, and religious spheres within a single interconnected civilization. Many believe that this can be accomplished through technological means—the invention of new organizational, political, and diplomatic instruments. Yes, it is clearly necessary to invent organizational structures appropriate to the multicultural age. But such efforts are doomed to failure if they do not grow out of something deeper, out of generally held values . . . .

Politicians at international forums may reiterate a thousand times that the basis of the new world order must be universal respect for human rights, but it will mean nothing as long as this imperative does not derive from the respect of the miracle of being, the miracle of the universe, the miracle of nature, the miracle of our own existence. Only someone who submits to the authority of the universal order and of creation, who values the right to be a part of it and a participant in it, can genuinely value himself and his neighbors and thus honor their rights as well.

The Declaration of Independence, adopted 218 years ago in this building, stated that the Creator gave man the right to liberty. It seems man can realize that liberty only if he does not forget the One who endowed him with it.

—excerpts from an address by Václav Havel, president of the Czech Republic, given in Independence Hall, Philadelphia, in July 1994

Hindu children and others learn South Indian classical dance in Birmingham, England

Needed: A Theology of Difference

Hans Ucko

The number of Muslims living in Europe is estimated at 24 million, which makes Islam numerically the second religion after Christianity. While countries of Eastern Europe (Bulgaria, Greece, Yugoslavia, Russia) have known Muslim fellow-citizens since the occupation by the Ottoman Empire in the sixteenth century, or the Russian colonization of the nineteenth century, the Muslim presence in countries of western Europe, such as Germany, France, and Belgium, results from the economic development of these countries, as well as from the economic, social, and political situation in the countries of origin of immigrants or those seeking asylum on political grounds. There are also large communities of Sikhs in Great Britain, and smaller communities of Hindus and Buddhists in many cities of Europe. Secularization is a problem within each religious community as is a tendency towards religious fundamentalism. Hans Ucko, in the article that follows, is in a unique position to assist churches in their reflection on this aspect of European life.

—Editor

Spiritual longing

Secularization does not automatically mean an end to the quest for the spiritual. Just because churches are empty does not mean that people's quest for the spiritual is dead and that only their craving for the material remains. There is a quest for the spiritual, but it is marginalized. It has difficulty expressing itself. It is afraid to use the language of the church, lest the church appropriate the quest and baptize it.

Jacques Delors, when he was president of the European Commission, has expressed something of the spiritual: "If in the next decade we fail to give Europe a soul, a spirituality, a meaning, we shall have lost the game." He goes on to say, "I hope that we can have contacts with the Catholic Church, the Protestant churches, the Jewish community, and even with the Muslims who are present among us. All these currents, all these forces must, I think, take an interest in the construction of the new Europe . . . a plan for civilization."

There are calls for rechristianizing Europe, for evangelizing the masses, for making Europe once again a Christian home. This kind of fundamentalism has its allies among other faiths in and near Europe. The conflicts between secularized Europeans and Muslims on women's wearing the *chadar*, the veil, testify to an inability to find a way to get along.

Many Muslim Europeans are growing insecure because of the eruption of racism in Germany with the burning of homes of Turks, many of them born in Germany. The seeming apathy of Christian Europe towards the plight of Muslims in Bosnia or towards the Palestinians in the West Bank and Gaza as compared with the zeal of the West to crush Iraq gives many Muslims reason enough to take refuge in a fundamentalist interpretation of Islam.

There is a task waiting for Christians in the new Europe. Hermann Goltz, writing on the Prague assembly of the Conference of European Churches, insists that "the churches have to find a way that will lead from the era of common statements into a future of common suffering for justice, for peace and for the integrity of cre-

Jewish children study the Torah *at a ḥeder in England*

ation. Needed is a theology of difference to facilitate ways of living together, sharing a common European home."

We cannot afford to define ourselves separated from the other, as integralists and nationalists propose. The presence in Europe of other faiths must be used as a building block in the construction of a new Europe. There are others willing to share in the construction of a pluralist, yet common European home.

Interreligious dialogue

There is today a dynamic process of interreligious understanding and cooperation going on. We see people of various faiths coming together to learn from each other as never before, cultivating a culture of dialogue, seeking ways of cooperation. Jewish-Christian dialogue is a remarkable example. As testimonies of a Christian commitment against anti-Semitism permeate the Jewish world, Jews have started to see Christians as possible partners in society.

Christian-Muslim dialogue knows a similar development. Christians and Muslims are cooperating in dealing with social issues, migrant workers, and refugees. They have met in Britain, France, and Germany, trying to counter outbursts of xenophobia and racism.

Interreligious dialogue is one significant and constructive alternative to atomization and religious fundamentalism. Through such dialogue, people of various religious traditions may find ways of ministering to the world, moving towards what the Jewish tradition calls *tikkun olam,* the mending of creation.

There is no particular Christian peace or Jewish justice or Muslim environmental policy. We live next door to each other as Jews, Christians, and Muslims in Europe. Through the encounter with the people of other faiths, we are exposed to a dimension of the truth that we do not know. This can be frightening. But we may also grow in our own faith.

We are compelled to come together with our distinct religious traditions, not to unite, not to merge, not to blend, but to affirm our differences, committing ourselves to a new attitude towards others. The concurrence of the richness of our religious traditions is needed in order to heal and mend Europe.

By streamlining our religious differences, we may arrive at a super-religion of universal love, global friendliness and cosmic consciousness, but it will be a religion similar to a concoction of ice cream and pudding. Easy to swallow, but of no substance.

We need to find, in the midst of our diversity, a possibility of affirming other faiths, of not allowing ourselves simply to think about ourselves, explaining the social world within our communities. We must break down the walls between our religious community and those outside it.

Tolerance will not suffice. We need to esteem people of other faiths. I am looking forward to the day when Christians will thank God that there are Muslims, Muslims will thank God for revealing Godself to Jews, Jews will thank God for the Christian way to God.

Hans Ucko is an executive secretary in the World Council of Church's Office on Interreligious Relations, based in Geneva. This article is excerpted from "The New Europe," which appeared in the June 1994 edition of One World.

Christian Women of Europe: 'Be Not Afraid'

Hedwig N. Lodwick

Under the dynamic theme, "Be Not Afraid—Remember the Future," the Ecumenical Forum of European Christian Women held its fourth assembly in Budapest, Hungary in August 1994. Three hundred women from Catholic, Orthodox, and Protestant women's organizations attended from twenty-eight countries.

Iris Kivimäki, press officer for the assembly, reported that for many eastern and central European Christian women this was the first opportunity to come together since the peaceful revolutions of 1989. Their hopes and problems are one of the biggest challenges for the future of the Forum. Women must

Helga Hiller

The Women's World Day of Prayer, which celebrated its 100th anniversary in 1987, is the largest ecumenical grassroots movement in Germany, with approximately 1.3 million women participating each year. Photo shows women of Kornwestheim, Germany, portraying women of Kenya and the burdens they carry for the 1991 theme "On the Journey Together."

reexamine their role in the new multicultural Europe and continue their struggle against violence and all forms of exclusion.

The delegates to the assembly know from their own experiences that Europe still lives in turmoil. The participation of women in the changes in society of the recent past was very important and remains even more so today as they "remember the future." The Forum continues its work through three working commissions: Peace and Justice, Bioethics and Ecology, and Theology and Spirituality, as well as in national and regional groups.

The Reverend Bärbel Wartenburg-Potter of Stuttgart, Germany, was one of the keynote speakers. She observed that while the Berlin Wall had fallen, many changes that followed were not those envisioned. Women in central and eastern countries used to employment, as well as guaranteed health and child care, were startled to find these no longer routinely available. While happy for better furnished markets and permission to travel, they began to wonder if it was necessary to lose that which they had considered good before. These women now question if they are winners or losers in the new Europe, and with society in general, feel they are wandering in the wilderness.

Rev. Wartenburg-Potter recalled that the freeing of the Israelites from the Egyptians did not lead immediately to the promised land, yet they did meet God in the wilderness. Dismay and confusion are felt in today's wilderness as concern mounts over the invasive market economy and its aggressive emphasis on profit over individual need, about the fear and nostalgia that has caused the violent return of nationalistic and ethnic forces and general rejection of aliens and asylum seekers. There is great concern about unemployment, the drug culture, AIDS, changes away from the traditional family, and about religious fanaticism, as well as the predominant secularism. Women have special reason to fear, for in times of upheaval they have always been among the first to be marginalized and victimized. Christians from mainline traditions also worry about the lack of active involvement of women in the churches of which they are nominal members.

To Christian women from such a variety of European countries, confessional communities, and situations, the Forum's message had deep significance. Wartenburg-Potter reminded the delegates that the Jewish-Christian tradition lives out of remembrance, it being the door to which we stride into the future. We remember God's paradise, the rainbow of the covenant, the picture of peace and justice embracing, and we direct ourselves to this light, believing with the prophet Ezekiel that dead bones can live again. The Bible calls us to bring our daily reality into the future of God's fullness and well being.

Genevieve Jacques, the General Secretary of CIMADE, a French Protestant ecumenical organization renowned for its work in saving lives in concentration camps during World War II and its current church-related emergency aid and migration work, reminded the women that times of crisis are also times of great opportunity. Today, more than in preceding generations, we have greater consciousness of the extreme complexities of the situations, problems, and interdependent relations between the large global questions. One sees the impossibility of isolating any question as number one, subordinating the others to it. It is the "complex interdependence of all the current issues which has become 'the vital problem' for us," she observed.

In past years, women of the Forum have reflected and learned from the story of the bent woman in

Bishop Maria Jepsen, North Elbian Evangelical Lutheran Church, Germany

Luke 13. They have seen that they too have been bent by sexism and patriarchal structures. But, said Wartenburg-Potter, "by Jesus' healing hand and our sisters, we have been helped to stand erect, to walk upright, and to use our voices. We have made our participation in church and society visible." Certainly in western Europe, women increasingly have studied theology and have joined the ordained clergy. The Lutheran Church in Germany was the first Lutheran church to ordain a woman as bishop. The prime minister of Norway and the president of Ireland are women, and there are senior women in the cabinets of other governments. Yet more needs to be done. Wartenburg-Potter continued her Bible study by saying women should now learn from the story of the woman in Luke 18 who with "impatient patience" worked toward her goal until she won what was right. However, when one is isolated or in a difficult environment, it is not easy to maintain courage, to imagine new responses. This is why encounters like those of the Forum are so important.

Special strengths

In 1982 when the Ecumenical Forum was established, women in the churches saw that ecumenical meetings involved mainly men as church leaders. Dr. Elisabeth Raiser, one of the outgoing presidents, said she believed this fact has been changing, in part, because of the Ecumenical Decade of the Churches in Solidarity with Women. Nevertheless, the Ecumenical Forum of European Christian Women still has particularities which underscore the importance of its separate existence. Elisabeth Raiser's list included the following observations: First, the Forum is independent of the churches. This makes it possible to speak to women who feel at home in their churches as well as to those who feel that they have no place in them. Second, the ecumenical nature of the Forum is greater than in other church organizations in that Catholic, Orthodox, and Protestant women have equal status. Finally, the self organization of women is simply quite other than in churches led by men. Much can be accomplished in very creative ways while joining women's strengths with others in the oikumene and walking with them in solidarity.

Raiser's thoughts, after four years sharing the co-presidency of the Forum, could be summed up in the affirmation, "Women don't want to build up a strict, dogmatic ecumenism, but to affirm diversity in the mosaic-like, scattered, and vulnerable Europe."

Three new co-presidents elected at the Budapest meeting are a Roman Catholic from England, an Orthodox from Finland, and a Baptist from Sweden. Their election and the actions of the Forum "encourages rich diversity rather than mono-dimensional unity . . . and presents a crossroads of views at a time when many Christian communities are defensive and cling to familiar identities through rearguard actions." No, the Ecumenical Forum of European Christian Women does not look backwards. It seeks to "remember the future" and to open ways forward. In a statement to the press, the Forum declared, "Mutual awareness of destructive forces that need to be faced and transformed is required if we would create a humane Europe with dignity for all its citizens. Helping to arm one another for the hard struggles of transformation, we recall our biblical theme: "Be Not Afraid." In closing, Genevieve Jacques challenged those at the Assembly to join the march, even though it leads through the wilderness. "It is urgent," she said. "We do not have time to be afraid. The future has already begun."

Hedwig N. Lodwick compiled and wrote this article from reports and speeches given at the General Assembly of the Ecumenical Forum of European Christian Women in Budapest, Hungary, August 19-26, 1994, and from her own experiences as a member of the Federation of Swiss Protestant Women and as an active participant in the work of the Ecumenical Forum.

A Letter to the Churches

Pasteur Jacques Stewart, President of the Protestant Federation of France, addressed a letter to member churches of the federation, a paragraph of which has been discussed by many persons across Europe:

"The International Year of the Family should be the occasion to recall that what is important for each one, is to be welcomed, accepted, adopted.... The true family is not just the natural family, that of blood or origin, but is the community, large or small, which welcomes, accepts, reconciles and integrates 'the other,' the stranger, those who come from the outside."

Encounter of Religions in the Black Sea Area

Earl A. Pope

Forty-two students from Russia, Ukraine and the Crimea, Moldova, Macedonia and Romania met together for the first time to participate in a seminar entitled "Encounter of Religions in the Black Sea Area," held at the Black Sea University, in Mangalia, Romania, in the summer of 1994. They represented Romanian Orthodox, Russian Orthodox, Jewish, Muslim, Baptist, Pentecostal, and Reformed communities and were primarily university students, many of whom were studying theology.

One of the primary objectives of the course was to initiate a dialogue among these religious communities so that they could better understand one another, shatter the ancient caricatures, and develop mutual respect and trust so as to become part of the solution rather than the problem.

Participants were invited to share their respective faith perspectives and to challenge one another in their search for peace and justice. It was emphasized that religious freedom could be used in positive ways and should not be perceived in a subversive manner and that each community had its own contributions to make in seeking to bring about the transformations so deeply needed both within and among their respective societies.

Earl A. Pope, Fulbright Professor of Religious Studies at the University of Bucharest, and co-director of this course, wrote this article for the Fall 1994 issue of CAREE Communicator.

Intentional Communities: Pilgrimages For Renewal

In 1995 many countries and millions of people will be celebrating the fiftieth anniversary of the end of World War II. In the summer of 1994, on the anniversary dates of D-Day and the Allied landings on the beaches of Normandy, many memories were recalled. From the ashes of that war, numerous forms of communities of religious renewal began to blossom, often around charismatic leaders such as Brother Roger in Taizé, France; George MacLeod in Iona and Glasgow, Scotland; and Chiara Lubich in Trent, Italy. Many seeds for these communities had been sown before 1945, but they developed more rapidly and along different paths in response to the search for a deepened spirituality, social justice, peace, and the renewal of the church.

The Iona Community

In 1938, as war clouds were gathering across Europe, the parish minister in a very congested corner of industrial Glasgow had a vision. Unemployment was a major concern in his part of the city. Some now-unknown parish saint suggested many unemployed persons could be used in rebuilding the ancient abbey on the island of Iona, which had been built by the Benedictines in the thirteenth century. Already by that time, Iona was known as a holy island, for Saint Columba had come there from Ireland on Pentecost day in 563 to begin a mission of the Celtic Church. Soon, Iona came to be recognized as the birthplace of Christianity

Abbey Church of St. Mary, Iona

© The Iona Community/Walter Rintoul

for much of Scotland, northern England, and Europe. Could the ruins be rebuilt and become a future witness in a modern secularized society?

Gingerly, George MacLeod, this young but bold Glasgow pastor, approached the committee that owned the abbey. In a letter he wrote some years later, he said:

To our surprise, they were delighted that we should have it. When we turned the page, they suggested we should find the money for the rebuilding! That summer a small group of workers went to the Island, at least to build two wooden huts, from which the builders might start rebuilding in earnest the permanent structure. But we were short of money. Then an unknown man in the local hotel wrote to *The Scotsman:* "Who are these, with their huts, ruining the Peace and Beauty of the Abbey?" Furthermore, he added, "They hang out their washing on a Sunday!" I was furious, but said nothing. A week later I got a letter from an unknown Scottish lady. Angry at the man, she wrote, "Why not hang out the washing? Is not cleanliness next to Godliness?" I turned over her letter . . . she wrote that she rejoiced in our building purpose . . . and enclosed a check for £10,000! How glad we were that the man from the hotel had criticized our washing!

Later in 1938 we really got started from the huts. But it was not a week before *The Scotsman* reported that, as the war had started, all timber in Britain was requisitioned for war purposes and we had no timber for the rebuilding. However, less than a week later, a ship coming over from Canada struck a storm just outside the Clyde. Her cargo was timber. This she jettisoned. It floated 80 miles . . . and landed on the coast of Mull opposite Iona . . . all the right length! It was from that moment that I knew God was on our side and the money would come and the Abbey would be completed.

Today, the Iona Community describes itself as "an ecumenical community of men and women, seeking new ways of living the Gospel in today's world. It has sought to be a sign of the rebuilding of the common life of the Church in the world, and to break down the barriers between prayer and politics, between the religious and the ordinary." The community is made up of approximately 200 members, 900 associates, and 2000 friends. The members are women and men, lay and ordained, working in different jobs and coming from many countries. There are fifty members, associates, and friends from the United States and Canada.

While the community came under the auspices of the Church of Scotland in 1952, its membership has always been open to members of other Christian denominations, and it has always welcomed to its centers on Iona and Mull people of all traditions and faiths, or of none. Members of the community live in varied locations throughout the United Kingdom and abroad and renew their commitment to the community on a yearly basis. They are bound together by a five-fold rule of prayer and Bible study, meeting together, accountability of the use of their time and money, and working for justice and peace.

The community maintains a resident group on Iona, to welcome the more than 100,000 visitors who come to the island each year. Hundreds come each week specifically to participate in the study and work program of the community. Many, if not a majority of these, are young people.

Worship is an essential component in the life of the community and is expressed in the worship book of the community in this way:

Worship is everything we do, both inside and outside the church. We begin each day with prayer together, common prayer, for we are a community, given to each other by God. In the morning service we do not end with a benediction, but simply with responses that prepare us to go straight out to the life of the world, there to continue worship in the context of our work. In the evening we come together again for common prayer, but we do not begin the service with a call to worship, for we have been at worship all day long. And only in the evening service do we have a final benediction at the close of the day.

In this symbolic way we try to express our conviction that the whole of our day is all of a piece, bracketed with common prayer, but continuing throughout every action of work and common life and recreation as one liturgy, one work of service offered to God.

—compiled from Iona publications

Ellsworth G. Stanton

George MacLeod

For decades, young people have thronged to Taizé, France

The Community of Taizé

I first visited the village of Taizé in 1948 as a college student following an ecumenical work camp at College Cevenol in Le Chambon-sur-Lignon, France. There were just a few brothers then gathered together in a village house and worshipping in the small Romanesque church, built in the twelfth century by monks of Cluny. Taizé is situated in Burgundy between Cluny and Citeaux. The Community of Taizé was unique in the 1940s as it was formed by a Swiss pastor of the National Protestant Church of Geneva, Roger Schutz, soon to be joined by another Genevan pastor, Max Thurian. Many Reformed Protestants wondered and still wonder what their great reformer, John Calvin, would have thought of this venture of two present-day pastors of his church. I think he would have given it his blessing in recognition of the blessing the community has been to others. Brother Roger became the prior of the community, a position he still holds today.

In a booklet about Taizé Brother Roger writes, "When I chose the hilltop village of Taizé in 1940, I was alone. The silence of the desert strengthens the encounter with God. Man alone with himself is sensitive to a presence alive within him. For a long period our life was marked not by isolation but by an accepted solitude. And yet, from the very start our life at Taizé has been interwoven by encounters with others. After twenty years of common life we were thrown, so to speak, into the public arena. It has taken us years to comprehend what was happening to us."

During the turbulent years of the sixties, young people all across Europe somehow heard about the Community of Taizé and came in droves, searching. They were searching for answers, for a spirituality they did not find in their own churches. They hungered for community. Brother Roger said, "While welcoming large numbers, we have always

found ways of establishing zones of peace on the hill. I suspect that simple values strengthen a creative capacity in us. And now young people from many different countries gather here, even in the depth of winter. These young people often have a great degree of selflessness. It comes from Christ. They shun privileges for themselves, and equally they cannot stand any caste mentality."

When I have returned to Taizé at different times over the years, it is not unusual during the summer months to see up to five thousand young people gathered on the hillside, living in tents, cooking the daily soup in giant cauldrons, sitting in small groups with one of the ninety or so brothers of Taizé discussing deep issues of faith. They seem not to be mindful of the rain or mud which are often present at various times of the year. At Easter as many as 25,000 young people have gathered there, seeking spiritual renewal. Years ago a new large church, called the Church of Reconciliation, had to be built to accommodate the crowds of worshippers. The little Romanesque church in the village is now a place of silence and prayer for the brothers. Whenever and wherever you see a young person wearing the Taizé cross you know that here is a kindred spirit.

Today, the community is truly ecumenical and international. There are Roman Catholic brothers, such as Brother Max, who joined the Roman Catholic Church a few years ago. There are critics of the community who believe Brother Roger has gone too far in accommodating to the Catholic Church in the life of the community, including its intense worship life. Yet, Brother Roger, a friend of Pope John Paul II and of most world religious leaders, believes that unity and reconciliation must go hand in hand.

"How can you anticipate a reconciliation?" Brother Roger asks.

By beginning to reconcile within yourself the best of the gifts God has placed in the Christian people during its 2,000-year-long pilgrimage. If you praise God for these gifts, you will be able to love them, and even go to the point of making them your own. On this path there is no danger of being a symbol of denial for your own people, nor of wounding the fibers of the soul in members of your own family of origin. You will discover the following and then put it into practice:

- Making your own the best of the gifts of the Orthodox churches means entrusting yourself to the joy of a presence—of the Risen Lord, and of the Holy Spirit.
- Making your own the best of the gifts of the churches of the Reformation means placing your confidence in the Word of God in order to put it into practice at once in your daily life.
- Making your own the best of the gifts of the Catholic Church means welcoming the irreplaceable presence of Christ in the Eucharist, welcoming it with the forgiveness given at the very source of reconciliation.

There are brothers in the community from many different countries and brothers who go out from the community in twos or threes to serve in difficult ministries among the destitute, from the inner city of New York to the ghettoes of Calcutta or Brazil, living a contemplative life among the poorest of the poor.

Part of the attraction to Taizé on the part of young people is Brother Roger's belief in them. He has said, "I would go to the ends of the earth if necessary, to the farthest reaches of the globe, to speak over and over again of my confidence in the new generations, my confidence in the young. We who are older have to listen, and not condemn. Listen, to grasp the creative intuitions alive within them. They are blazing trails, they are overturning barriers, they will take the whole People of God along with them. The young will find a way beyond the demarcation lines which now divide believers from believers, they will invent means of communion uniting believers with non-believers."

The Community of Taizé has become more than a community. It is a movement where young people feel empowered. The task is for that empowerment to be realized in the local congregations after one leaves the hill of Taizé and descends into everyday life. *Laudate omnes gentes, laudate Dominum* is a chant sung over and over again in the Church of Reconciliation and wherever Taizé friends gather. "All peoples, praise the Lord."

—Robert C. Lodwick
(quotes are from a Taizé publication entitled, *Taizé: Trust, Forgiveness, Reconciliation* by Brother Roger)

The Focolare Movement

In 1943 as bombs were falling, a young Italian woman, Chiara Lubich, with a group of friends, founded one of the most significant modern spiritual movements in Roman Catholicism. Called "Focolarini" by those who admired their spiritual warmth (from the Italian word for hearth), the Focolarini are not a Roman Catholic religious order like Jesuits or Franciscans, but a spiritual movement that includes laywomen and laymen, priests, bishops, and young people throughout the world. While remaining strictly Catholic themselves, the spirituality the Focolarini seek to live is itself profoundly ecumenical. In the past thirty years Focolare groups for Anglicans, Protestants, and Orthodox Christians have also been established.

For Chiara Lubich, the movement began in a very simple way in the town of Trent in northern Italy:

> We were very young and each of us had her own ideal in life. For one it was study, another saw her ideal in a future family, another in setting up a beautiful home; others found their ideal in art or in patriotism. But the war, with its air raids and bombs, destroyed more or less everything and prevented us from attaining the goals we had set for ourselves in life. One had to give up her studies; another's marriage could not take place as her fiance did not return from the front.
>
> It was as if circumstances themselves were teaching us a great lesson. Could there be an ideal that will not pass, an ideal that no bombs can destroy? And we saw at once that the answer was yes, there was such an ideal and that ideal was God! And so, together, we decided to put God in the first place in our lives. As we studied the gospel, we were struck forcibly by the words of Jesus, "Love one another as I have loved you." They seemed to us the synthesis of the whole gospel. It was like a dazzling revelation. We looked at one another and said "Let's try and live it! I will be prepared to die for you; you must be prepared to die for her; we must all be ready to die for one another." And we began to live in that way.
>
> This did not mean that God then asked us to die for one another literally, but many times God asked little things of us; for exam-

Chiara Lubich, founder of the Focolare Movement

> ple, to weep with someone who was weeping and to laugh with someone who was laughing, to share joys and sorrows, and to share our material and spiritual possessions. Our lives at that time were completely transformed. We saw in the gospel the code of life for the most fundamental, the most daring, the most far-reaching revolution for everyone in the world. So we began to take these words one by one and put them into practice.
>
> What did all this bring about? It guaranteed the presence of God in our midst and it was God who then spread the movement all over the world. Now, in fact, after more than fifty years, the diffusion of the movement can only be described as extraordinary. Today, the Focolare exists on all continents, its members, men and women of all vocations, are present in 160 different nations.

Gabriella Fallacara, of the ecumenical center of the Focolare Movement in Rome, continues:

> The Focolare movement was not born with a specific program in view but spontaneously, as a way of life based on the gospel and open to everyone. Within a few months, among more than five hundred families, the experience of the first Christian communities was repeated. Later, the first men's Focolare came into being. Each important develop-

ment, however, was submitted to the bishop so that nothing would develop that was not in full unity with the Roman Catholic Church. Some of the men in the Focolare began to feel a vocation to the priesthood. Among the married people who had welcomed this new spirit, there were some who felt they were called to the same life as the Focolare. As individuals they wanted to have the same commitments, compatible with their married state, but with the same total self-giving.

As the life of the movement spread spontaneously from Italy into Europe and then into five continents, at its heart other vocations came into light. Each person found his or her role at the service of the church and humankind.

Before 1960, as we were Catholics, and knew nothing at all about Christians of other churches and ecclesial communities, we thought that God had called the movement into being for the Catholic Church. None of us had thought about ecumenism. Then in 1960 we met some Lutheran friends. We told them our experiences and above all, we gave them our love. As they got to know us, they began to realize that this life was meant for them, too, because they saw it as a rediscovery of the gospel. With the permission of the competent authorities, a center was opened at Ottmaring, near Augsburg, Germany, where both Catholic and Lutheran Focolare communities live together. Later contacts were made with Anglicans and with Orthodox Christians.

One of the most well-known manifestations of the Focolare is the Mariapolis. These meetings bring thousands of people together in many places of the world in order to build and to experience for a few days the life of a Christian community. The permanent Mariapolis meeting places become small towns and are one of the most important visible expressions of this reality. They give a witness to life and are becoming a pole of attraction for many.

Chiara Lubich wants the Focolare to be engaged in four main areas of dialogue:

"There is the dialogue with the Catholic world where the movement makes its contribution to enable the church to become always more one in itself. There is the dialogue with the wider Christian world to contribute to its unification. There is the dialogue in the world of other religions, so that, getting to know and respect one another more, we might witness to and make known the God of Jesus Christ. Finally, in the secular world, there is a dialogue of working together with all of good will, where we work to build, consolidate, and extend the universal family."

In the United States and Canada there are over 80,000 persons associated with the Focolare Movement. Near Hyde Park, New York, the community has a 75-acre Mariapolis.

Excerpts from an interview with Chiara Lubich were chosen and updated by Gabriella Fallacara and published in Chiara Lubich: Life for Unity *by Franca Zambonini (New Rochelle, NY: New City Press, 1992).*

The Quest for Spiritual Fathers

Increasing numbers of people in the Orthodox churches in Europe are looking for a spiritual father who will not simply act as their confessor, but will be able to inspire and guide them in their lives. There are many priests who are capable of such a mission, but demand still outstrips supply. In addition to their ordinary parish responsibilities, most of these priests spend long hours hearing confessions, leading and advising groups of young people, and taking part in a host of other activities. Often they show signs of exhaustion, but people expect them always to be present and always strong.

But where people literally throng is to certain places where there are great spiritual fathers, towering figures who often combine the gifts of discernment and healing with their personal holiness and wisdom. In the Balkans there are alive today more than ten such figures who are known throughout the region, spread over all the major Orthodox countries. These people are considered contemporary saints. There are certainly others less known or unknown.

I had the good fortune to know personally the elder Porphyrios, who died in 1992. The elder lived in Malakasa, about an hour's drive from Athens. He had severe health problems and was not always able to receive the people who arrived by dozens or even hundreds every day. Each one of them was expecting advice on some serious problem, a prayer from the elder, or just a blessing. The elder had the gift of discernment, and performed many miracles of healing. Not only are these gifts widely known, but I can vouch for them myself.

Things like this come as a surprise to Athenians who have been brought up on rationalism. The elder had very little education, but he could speak to his visitors on technical or scientific or medical matters with amazing precision. He was approachable, and not at all severe. I remember asking him as a child of twelve how one could expel evil thoughts from one's mind, and he answered, "Can you chase the darkness out of a darkened room? However much you blow, however much you try, you won't manage it. But open a window to let the light in, and then you'll see that the darkness will take flight. So you do the same: Don't concentrate on the darkness. Look at Christ, think about Him all the time as if you are in love; then you'll see that the evil thoughts will disappear on their own."

I know now that he often taught the same thing, just as he often told parents not to put pressure on their children. Having foreseen his own death, he left his disciples a short letter before he died in which his main commandment was to think of Christ constantly and to study and imitate the lives of the saints. Even today, in times of spiritual conflict and trouble, I think of the elder Porphyrios with his inner peace and his love for Christ, and his simple words which always had a beneficial effect in my life.

I would also like to mention the tremendous influence today of the Holy Mountain, Mount Athos. Geographically it is part of Greece, but is administratively independent under the ecclesiastical jurisdiction of the Ecumenical Patriarchate. The splendid natural location of the Athos peninsula, with a diversity of flora among the richest in the world, has been inhabited by ascetics from ancient times. The first community was founded in 963 by St. Athanasius of Athos. Other monasteries followed and to this day it is the most important international center of Orthodox monasticism. The Athonite monasteries represent a very ancient monastic tradition. From very early on they exerted considerable influence throughout the Balkans. During the Turkish period, the Holy Mountain provided spiritual support for those who suffered under the occupation.

Today on the Holy Mountain there are twenty monasteries: Greek, Russian, Serbian, Bulgarian, and Romanian make up the sacred community. Almost all of them are communal in their organizations. The ascetics and hermits who live on their own also belong to one or another monastery. Many monasteries have monks from Western Europe, North and South America, Asia, and Australia. The average age is lower than in the past due to many younger monks coming to Mount Athos.

No women, even female animals, are allowed on Mount Athos, for the Holy Mountain is for men only. Thousands of male visitors, Greeks and foreigners, Orthodox and non-Orthodox, come to the mountain every day. In recent years, the crowds have been so large that officials have been forced to receive visitors in order of priority, which is very unpopular with those who have a burning desire to go there but are hampered by limited time. Of late, Athonite monks have been sought after as speakers in the universities and startle students with their anti-conformist simplicity, their non-rationalist but extremely modern spirit, and their profound spiritual experience.

—Evi Voulgaraki-Pissina, translated by Elizabeth Theokritoff

Moment of confession at All Saints, Akademgorodok, Russia

Eastern Europe

Leonid Kishkovsky

The New Commonwealth: Image and Reality

What images come to mind when you think of Russia and the other countries of the Commonwealth of Independent States? (The CIS includes all the former republics of the Soviet Union with the exception of the three Baltic nations: Estonia, Latvia, and Lithuania.) Nationalism in resurgence. Political conflict. Crime. The emergence of capitalism. Social dislocation and poverty. New freedom and the collapse of totalitarianism. The reemergence of communist parties under new labels. A struggle for democracy and democratic institutions. These images, as contradictory as they are, represent aspects of the reality.

From time to time, another set of images emerges in our media. Children lighting candles in newly reopened churches in Russia. The patriarch of Moscow, as leader of the Russian Orthodox Church, acting as a mediator in the conflict between president and parliament. Eastern-rite Catholics in conflict with the Orthodox in Ukraine. Protestant mission activities in the Russian Federation threatened by legislation in the Russian parliament. The religious aspect of the conflict between (Muslim) Azerbaijan and (Christian) Armenia.

It is important for Christians and other citizens in the United States and Canada to understand this second set of images. We need to understand the textures of daily life in Christian communities and to examine an overview of the larger issues in the part of eastern Europe and Asia called the Commonwealth of Independent States.

The legacy of communism

One of the central and constant features of communist theory and practice was hostility to religion. This hostility was expressed in a variety of ways. In the Soviet Union there were periods of genocidal violence against religion. In Russia (and the Soviet Union) the largest single religious community was the Russian Orthodox. During the 1920s and 1930s dozens of Russian Orthodox bishops and thousands of priests and monastics (monks and nuns) were imprisoned, exiled, and killed, as were tens of thousands of lay people. The Russian Orthodox Church lost almost all of its nearly 60,000 churches during this period. Churches were confiscated and turned into public toilets, warehouses, offices, workshops, plants, and museums.

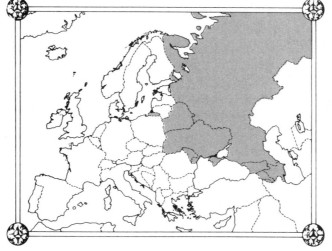

Often, churches were simply destroyed.

By the late 1930s, there were only several hundred Russian Orthodox churches open for worship in the whole Soviet Union. During World War II the Soviet regime, by decision of Joseph Stalin, permitted the reopening of churches as a measure to encourage the patriotic feelings of the population during the war against Nazi Germany. Thus, in the late 1940s and early 1950s there were some fourteen thousand Russian Orthodox churches open for worship. Then, in the late 1950s and early 1960s, the regime of Nikita Khrushchev launched anti-religious campaigns that resulted in the closing of approximately half of the Russian Orthodox churches. In 1988, on the threshold of the collapse of the Soviet Union (and during the celebration of the one-thousandth anniversary of Christianity in Russia, Ukraine, and Belarus), there were only some seven thousand Russian Orthodox churches available for worship.

The same treatment was given to other Christian communities and to other religions. The Orthodox churches of Georgia and Armenia, the Roman Catholic and Protestant churches, and the Jewish, Muslim, and Buddhist communities also suffered intense persecution and oppression.

The only legally permissible activity of the religious communities under Soviet communism was public worship in the officially registered places of worship. The life and public witness of religion was confined to the church buildings. Everything else was forbidden—religious education for children or adults, parish libraries, publications, charitable work, hospital visits, mission outreach. Only a very limited number of Bibles could be printed when paper was received as a gift from northern European countries in the mid-1980s.

In the public arena, religion and religious believers were subjected to constant assault and caricature. The educational system, the press and other mass media, were active propagandists for atheism and against religious faith. No one identified as a religious believer had any possibility of career advancement. In some professions, to be identified as a religious believer meant to lose your job.

> It is not a simple matter to emerge from the ghetto. For some, the greatest temptation is passivity. For others, it is activism.

The decades of oppression and persecution have placed the Russian Orthodox Church and the other churches and religious communities in a paradoxical situation. Martyrdom is understood by Christians as a source of spiritual strength and vitality. The old Christian saying expresses this best: "The blood of the martyrs is the seed of the church." Martyrdom has given credibility to the Russian Orthodox Church. At the same time, the institutional life of the church was terribly weakened by decades of oppression. Its institutional capacity to respond effectively to the new freedoms and challenges is weak.

While the Russian Orthodox Church has restored or constructed at least eight thousand churches since 1989, there are many more congregations waiting for the return of church property or preparing to build a church on a new site when permission is given and material resources are in hand. However, the church is the first to admit it faces shortages in every aspect of its life. There are not enough clergy, teachers, theologians, or books and religious education materials. There is a lack of financial resources as the demands on the church escalate and the population becomes more impoverished. The same paradox of strength and weakness is faced by the other Christian communities and by the other religions.

Another legacy of communism that affects the society as a whole, as well as the religious communities, is the tenacity of old habits and old fears. It is not a simple matter for the religious communities to emerge from the marginalized ghetto to which they were consigned in Soviet society. For some, the greatest temptation is passivity. They have internalized the limitations of the past, have made these limitations their own, and therefore cannot address the challenges of today. For others, the greatest temptation is activism. They jump at the new opportunities to act in the public arena but make the mistake of tying their religious faith too closely to social and political agendas of the moment. Thus, in the Russian Orthodox Church some are too involved in nationalist causes, while others are too caught up in radical democratic activism.

Bishop Forgon Pal of Berogrova, Ukraine; scrapbook contains messages he sent home during five years of exile in Siberia

The major Christian tradition in the countries today comprising the Commonwealth of Independent States has been and is the Orthodox. In Russia, Ukraine, Belarus, Moldova, and Georgia, the Eastern Orthodox have been the majority; in Armenia, the Oriental Orthodox Armenian Church has formed the national consciousness and culture. In the Central Asian nations, where Islam is the predominant religious presence, the major Christian presence has been Orthodox. Baptists and Lutherans have been present in Russia since the eighteeth century, and Methodists and Pentecostals also have a presence. However, these groups are small minorities in an Orthodox milieu.

Thus, the Christians of North America are challenged to understand Christian histories and traditions very different from their own, if they want to understand the region we now call the Commonwealth of Independent States. In Canada and the United States the predominant Christian communities are Protestant, Anglican, and Roman Catholic. All of these, with due respect to the differences among them, are still part of the great Western Christian tradition. In the nations of the CIS, the churches of the Western tradition are small minorities, and the Eastern Christian tradition as represented by the Russian Orthodox Church is the historic form of Christianity.

The Orthodox churches have been culture-creating and nation-building forces in the histories of their peoples. This is true especially of Russia, Georgia, and Armenia, where the language, music, architec-

ture, literature, and folk piety of each has been greatly influenced, even shaped, by the Orthodox Church. This means that the moral values of these peoples have also been inspired and shaped by the Orthodox Church.

In such historical contexts it would be foolish to expect that the Orthodox Church could step back from its historic role to become simply one among many religious communities. In terms of constitution and law it is, of course, important, even essential, that there be equality of religious communities. In terms of history and cultural impact, it is obvious that the Orthodox Church has a special role in Russia, Georgia, Armenia, Belarus, Moldova, and Ukraine.

Take, for example, the events of September–October 1993 in Moscow. The conflict and standoff between the parliament and the presidency had reached a point of explosion. The only institution both sides could accept as a credible mediator was the Russian Orthodox Church. Patriarch Alexy II of Moscow personally took upon himself the task and the burden of the mediation effort. Ultimately, the mediation failed. There was violence and bloodshed. First, armed mobs inspired by the parliament leaders attacked in Moscow, rampaging through the Moscow streets. Then the armed forces, in support of the presidency, fired on the White House, then the parliament building of the Russian Federation. They occupied the building and arrested the parliamentari-

Awaiting confirmation in a Ukrainian village—the first in 40 years

63

Restoration to reclaim St. Peter's Church, Moscow

'Swimming Pool Church' to Serve as Cultural Center

St. Petersburg's "swimming pool church," St. Peter's, will be restored and used as a cultural center, not only for the German Lutheran congregation but also for the general public. A meeting place has been installed on the upper floor, while the office of the bishop of the Evangelical Lutheran Church in Russia and Other States is located in the former sauna. On Sundays, the Lutheran services in Russian and German still take place in St. Anne's Church, which has been a cinema complex since the 1950s.

Before the revolution of 1917, there were fourteen Lutheran churches of all nationalities in St. Petersburg. St. Peter's Church on Newskiy Prospect was built in the years 1832-1838 to replace an older edifice. In 1937, the church was closed by the Soviet state and in the 1950s turned into a swimming pool. Giant diving platforms were installed where the altar stood, and instead of the galleries there were spectator stands. Only when the swimming pool went bankrupt in August 1992, and after several months of negotiations, was the building given back to the Lutherans. The first service took place in June 1993.

Today the German Lutheran congregation in St. Petersburg has almost 700 members, who are actively involved in the reconstruction of St. Peter's, now, ironically, classified as a historic monument. An architect who was involved in building the swimming pool in the 1950s is now an adviser for the renovation.

—Reprinted by permission from
Lutheran World Information

ans and others implicated in the armed uprising. The violence was dangerous and tragic. Yet Russia did not descend into general civil war. There are some in Russia today who say that civil war was forestalled by the mediation effort of the Russian Orthodox Church. And even if the goal of the mediation—prevention of all violence—was not reached, it is certainly significant that both sides in the conflict regarded the church as a legitimate arbiter.

Some political commentators in North America and Western Europe see religion in today's world as part of the problem, but not part of the solution, in the contemporary world scene. They see central and eastern Europe, including Russia and the other CIS nations, in this light.

It is, indeed, sadly true that there are leaders and movements misusing the religious motive, adding religious energy to the political and ethnic fires that have been set ablaze. In the conflict between Armenia and Azerbaijan it is unquestionably true that religious history and religious memory add fuel to the fires of hatred. On the Armenian side, there is memory of Islamic domination and terror imposed on subject Armenians by dominant Islam through the centuries. On the side of Azerbaijan, there is a sense of Islamic confrontation with Christianity.

Peacemaking efforts

In light of the above, it is all the more important to understand that the serious efforts at making peace have emerged from within the religious communities, both Christian and Islamic. One of these religious initiatives towards the cessation of the violence and the making of peace came from the Russian Orthodox Church and its patriarch, Alexy II. In 1993 the religious leaders of Islam in Azerbaijan and the religious leaders of the Armenian Church came together in Moscow at the invitation of Patriarch Alexy II. They issued an appeal to the political leaders of the countries to bring to an end the violence, in which great suffering is inflicted on innocent and peaceful people on both sides.

Another religious initiative towards the building of civil society and the avoidance of civil conflict and violence took place in June 1994 in Moscow. The Russian Orthodox Church, joined by the Orthodox Churches of Georgia and Armenia, and together with the Roman Catholic and Protestant churches of Russia, convened a conference on "Christian Faith and Human Enmity." The purpose of the conference was to give the opportunity to the main Christian confessions in the Russian Federation, and in the other independent states of the Commonwealth of Independent States and the Baltic region, to come together in order to address the threats of ethnic tensions and national enmity. The examples of the violence in the Balkans, in the Caucasus, in Central Asia, and in Moldova have made it clear that the Christian communities must bear witness together to the urgent need for peace and tolerance, for mutual respect, forgiveness, and reconciliation. Because the Christian communities are living side by side with people of other religions, such as Jews, Muslims, and Buddhists, guests representing these religions participated in the Moscow conference as observers. However, their status was not that of silent guests; rather, they were invited to speak to the issues before the conference.

Significantly, the worldwide ecumenical Christian fellowship provided moral and financial support to the conference. As a sign of this support, representatives of the National Council of the Churches of Christ in the USA, the Conference of European Churches, the Council of European Bishops' Conferences (Roman Catholic) as well as the Vatican itself, and the World Council of Churches were present and participated in the conference. Financial support for the conference represented unique ecumenical cooperation among U.S. Protestants, Roman Catholics, and Orthodox, and also unique cooperation between the religious community and public organizations. Grants were received from the International Orthodox Christian Charities, from Protestant and Orthodox member churches of the National Council

Wedding lunch at Evangelical Lutheran Church of Ingria in Kelton, Russia

of Churches, from the Roman Catholic Church, and from World Vision. From the public sector, grants were received from the National Endowment for Democracy and the Eurasia Foundation.

The conference appeal (see page 68) addresses the challenges that are faced in the region. It tries to give a sign that the Christian churches and communities are coming together to challenge and assist their societies to resolve conflicts in a nonviolent way.

It is important also that a "continuation committee" has been endorsed and established. In this committee the churches will maintain contact and stay in conversation with one another, will share information, and will work out mechanisms for cooperative action. It was clearly envisioned that this Christian committee will be open to regular dialogue and cooperation on matters of mutual concern with other religions. At a time of extreme danger and in the face of threats of intolerance and violence, the Christians in the Eurasian region have been able to give a sign of Christian peacemaking.

The future of mission

Communist totalitarianism was a closed society. Tight controls imposed by the Communist Party state through a repressive secret police apparatus characterized the social and political system. In the public arena, the controls were total and effective. In the private arena, which the communist state also tried its best to control, some people secretly practiced their faith and values against the overwhelming pressure of the atheist propaganda apparatus.

When the closed society broke down, freedom became a reality quickly. Religious freedom meant

Music class at seminary in Smolensk, Russia

that religious belief could be publicly manifested, that churches could engage in mission, education, and charity. Political freedom and freedom of the press meant that clashing political viewpoints could be expressed in the political struggles, that varying worldviews could be reflected in the press.

Freedom becoming reality did not mean that society and citizens were ready for freedom. Abuses of freedom emerged all too quickly. In the marketplace of ideas some ideas propagated hatred, intolerance, chauvinism. Other ideas came under the guise of the "new" but actually propagated hatred and derision of religious faith, thus continuing the work of the old atheism. Yet other ideas used religion and faith to give energy to unworthy and narrow-minded social and political ideologies, whether nationalist (of the reactionary type) or anti-foreign, or a combination of communism and nationalism.

Aggressive mission activity

With the emergence of the new freedom, the way was opened to new activities, new movements, new phenomena in the life of society. Quickly enough religious movements around the world saw the territories of the former Soviet Union as open mission territory. Some of the mission activities have been aggressive, high-profile, culturally insensitive. Some of those involved in such activities have assumed that they were bringing the gospel of Christ to peoples who had never heard it. New religious movements had been almost totally unfamiliar in communist societies, and their appearance on the scene was a social shock.

In several instances, new Christian groups and groups from the new religious movements have obtained special privileges from the state. For example, in the Russian Federation, the Ministry of Education has given ready access to the public schools and to the public school curriculum to CoMission, a cooperative U.S.-based evangelical Christian educational program (with strong participation from Campus Crusade for Christ). In yet another example, the same Ministry of Education has given access to the public schools to the Unification Church (the so-called Moonies). The Russian Orthodox Church has on a number of occasions worked with the CoMission program, and CoMission has been open to cooperation with the Orthodox Christians and other Christians of Russia. Cooperation with the Unification Church, of course, does not and cannot enter into the minds of Christian communities in

Thanksgiving service for WCC Central Committee, 1989, at Russian Orthodox Church monastic center of Zagorsk

Russia. To Russian citizens it seems that the agreements of the Ministry of Education with various foreign religious groups represent the selling of the souls of Russian children to foreign religious groups and cults.

In this context, what responsible Christian churches and programs are doing and propose to do in Russia and other postcommunist societies has also become a sensitive issue. It is critically important that U.S. and Canadian churches acquire the necessary knowledge about the historical and cultural contexts of the nations of central and eastern Europe. In the case of historically Orthodox countries, understanding of the Eastern Christian tradition is obviously important. And above all, cooperative work with the Christian churches and communities who have witnessed and suffered under the recent communist oppression is surely the honorable and Christian way towards mission. The competitive, aggressive way of doing mission while ignoring the experience and historic presence of Orthodox, Roman Catholic, and Protestant churches in the region does not do honor to the gospel and indeed does violence to effective mission. (See related article on page 72.)

The witness of worship

The story of Christianity in Russia and other postcommunist societies is really the story of the revival of mission and ministry in the parish setting. To put it another way, it is the revival of the parish as community for mission.

It must be said, first, that under communist persecution and oppression, it was worship and the worshipping community that bore witness to the gospel, thus accomplishing the task of mission. The materialist, atheist ideology of communism presumed that worship of a (nonexistent) God was the one activity of Christians that was most certainly senseless and without any possible impact on the society and on modern humanity. Therefore, worship could be permitted under strictly controlled circumstances. Ironically, it was precisely worship that was the most powerful witness to the gospel of Christ, to the cross of Christ, and to the resurrection of Christ in conditions of totalitarian oppression.

The parish and congregation, limited exclusively to worship, were real communities in the sense that prayer, especially the prayer of the oppressed, builds community and nourishes God-given dignity. For the Orthodox, the powerful spiritual reality was the existence of the church as eucharistic community. Yet it must also be said that the parish, under communism, could not nurture the spirit of common life through common mission and ministry in the world. There was a strong sociological and psychological pressure that forced people to be isolated individuals, rather than members of community, in the parish setting. People would participate in services, and would know that they were part of the church on earth and the church in heaven glorifying God, but they would not interact with one another in the parish setting outside of worship.

Illegal seminars

In some instances, small cells of Christian community were created. These were illegal and underground. Young parents would come together in small groups to provide Christian education for their children. Sometimes a priest would join them to lead them in prayer, and even in eucharistic celebration. Small seminars for adults seeking religious knowledge were created, and sometimes these worked for years without being discovered. When discovered, such efforts at the building of Christian community resulted in the arrest and imprisonment of the seminar leaders.

Even before the complete collapse of the communist political system of the Soviet Union, in the later years of the rule of President Mikhail Gorbachev, parish life began to emerge from its social straitjacket. With the full emergence of religious freedom in the late 1980s or early 1990s, parish life came into its own.

We must not underestimate the difficulties and obstacles that stand in the way of this revival of parish community. Old habits die hard. Clergy are overwhelmed by baptisms, confessions, and worship services, and find it difficult to allocate time for the building of parish community. Trained and experienced lay leaders do not exist.

And yet, in parish after parish, there is indeed a real revival of parish as community for ministry and mission. What is most impressive about this revival is its sense of sanity and balance. When a ruined church building is returned to church use, it would be understandable if the main thrust of parish life would be the restoration of the church building. In the present conditions of economic hardship and poverty, the restoration of churches alone is a heroic project. Yet in parish after parish there is a remarkable catholicity of approach to the question of parish life. The education of children and adults is given high priority. Public lectures for seekers are offered. There are ministries of outreach providing visits to the shut-ins, to the hospitalized, to the institutionalized. The image of Orthodoxy as an exclusively liturgical church, with little social conscience, is today simply a false image in Russia and in other nations of the CIS.

The Russian Orthodox Church is the largest nongovernmental organization in the Russian Federation. The same can be said about the Orthodox Churches in Ukraine, Belarus, Moldova, Georgia, and Armenia. The parish renewal of which we have spoken here is thus not only a matter of building up church structures. It is a matter of building up civil society at the ground level. Even more important, it is a matter of the spiritual renewal of nations and peoples who are today threatened by new forms of idol worship, new forms of injustice, and new forms of intolerance.

Father Leonid Kishkovsky is the ecumenical officer of the Orthodox Church in America, former president of the National Council of the Churches of Christ in the USA, current chair of the Europe Committee of the NCCC-USA, and a member of the Central and Executive Committees of the World Council of Churches. He has had long and close contacts with the Russian Orthodox Church and the Orthodox and Protestant churches of the Commonwealth of Independent States.

Appeal on 'Christian Faith and Human Enmity'

St. Daniel's Monastery, Moscow, June 21-23, 1994

As peoples of the CIS and the Baltic states are building their statehood, they learn to live under new historical conditions. Their learning is not without mistakes since the grave legacy of the past and the present generation's lack of experience of peaceful, free and responsible renewal of life have led to the aggravation of enmity among people of various nationalities, cultures, and worldviews. Everywhere in our countries social and political tensions have increased and bloody conflicts have broken out.

Being aware of our responsibility before God and people, we, Orthodox, Catholics, and Protestants serving God in the CIS and in the Baltic states, have agreed to make a new beginning in our common work to put an end to the God-defying violence so that peace with justice and accord could be established in our lands.

"Do not be overcome by evil, but overcome evil with good" (Rom. 12:21)—may these words be our motto now on our path to reconciliation. Today the duty of all those who follow Christ is to oppose war, violence and enmity with the works of love and peace.

Thus, we resolutely urge the state authorities and peoples of our countries to stop all the fratricidal strife in the territory of the CIS through reasonable concessions and compromises, among other means. We invite all those involved in conflicts and disputes to solve them only through dialogue taking into account the aspirations of all parties seeking a solution of the conflicts. We believe that in order to reduce interethnic, intercultural, social and civil tensions it is necessary that every member of society should realize his duty to treat people of other nationalities, social groups, cultures, faiths, political convictions with love and respect, to help them no less than the people of the same background, faith and convictions, not to allow the poor and the sick to be rejected, to promote just economic order and to actively oppose any manifestations of hatred and enmity which divide people. Fully aware of the important role played by the mass media in the world today, we call upon them to promote reconciliation and to oppose enmity.

We share the commitment to generally accepted principles of respect for human rights, including the right to the freedom of conscience and equality of people of different nationalities, religious and other convictions before law. We are profoundly concerned over violations of human rights today.

Without replacing the efforts undertaken by the states and without getting involved in political struggle, Christian churches and religious associations will do whatever possible to help reconcile those who are at enmity in order to establish peace and accord in our countries. At the same time, we are convinced that today it is only together that we can serve the cause of reconciliation and realizing this we have agreed that it would be useful to ensure regular coordination of our religious and social actions and to maintain dialogue for overcoming problems emerging both among Christians and in their relations with the world around them. In our service to society we are open to cooperation with the followers of other religions.

We pray to our One Lord and Savior of Humanity Christ that He may grant to statesmen and peoples of our countries peace, wisdom, and success in every good undertaking. O Lord, hear our prayer!

Work camp participants at St. Dmitri Prilutsky Monastery, Vologda

Ecumenical Work Camp in Russia

Joan Löfgren

Opportunities for young people to learn about church life in Russia have kept pace with the sweeping changes taking place there. The Europe Office of the National Council of the Churches of Christ in the USA has sponsored ecumenical young adult work camps in Russia since 1990, in cooperation with the All-Church Orthodox Youth Movement based in Moscow. The three-week program, usually held in August, combines preparatory readings, orientation, renovation of monasteries, convents and churches, and touring of historical and cultural sites. Work camp groups involve two leaders/translators and about twenty young adults, primarily 18 to 30 years old, from churches in the United States and Canada.

The Russia work camps have taken place in Volokolamsk, the Smolensk region, Vologda, and Kostroma. Altogether over one hundred young adults have been involved. Work projects have included clearing out debris from a cathedral undergoing renovation, restoring a cemetery in ruin, preparing a dairy barn and hay for winter use by a convent, and restoring a cemetery. Restoring the cemetery of the Prilutsky Monastery was an especially poignant task. It had been left in total ruin by the Soviet military forces, which had occupied the monastery and used it as a prison since the 1920s. Participants became aware of the need to remember all those whose lives ended in persecution and the deep need for reconciliation in this post-Soviet era.

Participants have brought back from Russia a wide range of valuable experiences, including:

- a broader understanding of the history and culture of Russia, through personal preparation and their own encounter with Russian society;
- a new perspective on the persecution of the churches in the Soviet era, while working with the tangible signs of their suffering;
- a deeper respect for Russian Orthodoxy and their own spirituality, as they struggled with differences between Orthodox and Protestant liturgies and theology;
- a taste of daily life in Russia, seeing it and experiencing it for themselves. "Living in one place for ten days, one can learn more than all the touring in the world," one participant remarked.
- a glimpse of rural life in Russia, where the large-hearted hospitality of the Russian people shines through;
- an appreciation for the challenges facing young people in Russia today, amidst an influx of Western culture and values;
- an opportunity to overcome misunderstandings between churches in East and West perpetuated by the Cold War.

As one participant reflected, "Doing achieves more than saying or promising. We have 'done' and must continue to do so!"

Joan Löfgren, a Ph.D. candidate at Columbia University, has assisted the NCCC-USA Europe office with its travel programs and has led the work camps in Russia.

One Woman's Search Leads Others to Christ

Leonid Kishkovsky

Natalya Gorelova is one of the many laywomen and laymen in the Russian Orthodox Church today who are instrumental in the revival of the church and in the hope of renewal for the whole society. Created to be a "city without God," the parish in Akademgorodok is a witness to God's living and active presence in the city and surrounding region.

Akademgorodok, a town fifteen miles from the old Russian city of Novosibirsk, is a city created from the birch forests by the Soviet regime to be the primary scientific research center of the Soviet Union. It was a city of pure science and scientific experimentation; no churches existed there, and no churches were ever supposed to exist.

When, in the late 1980s religious liberty slowly emerged in the Soviet Union, people of Akademgorodok applied for permission to build a church in December 1989. The necessary permits were given by the city authorities, and a church community quickly formed. The first Holy Liturgy took place in June 1990. The service occurred in a cathedral where the walls were made of live birch trees and the dome of which was the very sky. The next order of priority was to build a log church. The small wooden church was built in 1991 with a belfry and seven silver domes, and next to it a log cabin for Sunday School classes. The church was consecrated "All Saints Who Illumined the Russian Land."

One of the lay leaders in the parish is Dr. Natalya Gorelova, a mathematician and geologist. She was born in Siberia, studied at Moscow State University, and in 1971 was sent to Akademgorodok to do postgraduate work in cybernetics. She has three children, a grown-up son and two teenage daughters.

Natalya was baptized in infancy, but did not cross a church threshold in her younger years. She has said that she always knew that God exists, and prayed every night (although she did not call this "prayer" until she was an adult). She points out that there is a distinction between coming to God and coming to Christ. She read deeply in existentialist philosophy and eastern religions, but remained unsatisfied and restless spiritually. Then, in a book about cybernetics, she read about Christ. A saying of Jesus Christ was used by the author to illustrate negative and positive feedback. "If anyone strikes you on the right cheek, turn the other also"

Students at the Orthodox school in Akademgorodok, Novosibirsk, hold model of what they hope one day will be the Siberian Religious Center. At left is Natalya Gorelova, principal.

(Matt. 5:39). This statement, wrote the author, can be explained mathematically. If you retaliate, evil for evil, you increase the amount of evil. By refusing to retaliate, you decrease the amount of evil.

Natalya's spiritual search led her into the Orthodox Church after a long journey. Her first Bible came to her from the Baptists, but she did not feel at home in the Baptist Church. At first she was drawn to the Orthodox Church intellectually, through reading about the liturgy and the sacraments. Then, on a visit to a Moscow church, she was introduced to confession and holy communion by the loving attention given to her by some of the grandmothers, or *babushkas*.

Her conversion had an impact on many other people, including many of her more than forty godchildren, some of whom are archeologists, biologists, and mathematicians.

By 1993 over 12,000 persons had been baptized into this new congregation. In 1990 there were only nine churches in the Novosibirsk diocese; today there are more than 100. The parish is actively engaged in educational and social work, reaching out to people and their spiritual and material needs.

In 1992, the parish established a "gymnasium" or high school, which offers a full education centering on the confession and practice of the Christian faith. Natalya became the principal of this high school, which was the first non-governmental secondary school to be opened under the direction of the church in the Novosibirsk diocese. The high school has been named "Saint Sergius of Radonezh Orthodox Gymnasium."

Scenes from the Church of All Saints Who Illumined the Russian Land in Akademgorodok, Novosibirsk. Above, confession; below, Mother Najesta and Archpriest Boris; below right, baptism.

71

Proselytism Damages Church Relations

Robert C. Lodwick

WCC Central Committee at service in Moscow Baptist Church, 1989

Pros-e-ly-tize: 1. to try to convert (a person), especially to one's religion. 2. to persuade to do or join something, especially by offering an inducement.

The reader will soon discover in articles on eastern Europe and the Balkans the difficult issue of proselytism, which has severely damaged ecumenical relations in those countries during the past five years. Proselytism is not a new issue in the Orthodox world, for in the Middle East it has been an irritant or stumbling block for decades between Protestant and Catholic missions and the ancient Orthodox churches.

Within the Orthodox world of eastern Europe, particularly during the past half century under Communist restrictions, the movement of Western mission agencies or parachurch groups was severely limited. An underground movement of Bible smuggling and clandestine meetings with certain clergy and lay groups did exist, and when there were extreme shortages of medicines or other necessary goods it seemed possible to have a border guard look

the other way in exchange for a small but precious bottle of aspirin.

However, after the peaceful revolution of 1989, hundreds of persons and groups rushed in "to bring the gospel" to those who lived under the atheist Communist repression. Preaching to an overflow Baptist congregation of believers, one American evangelist addressed them as "You who have been without the good news of Christ for 70 years . . ." Yet they had been faithful and knew the price of that faithfulness in a way never experienced by that evangelist! More often than not, these groups set up their mission operations without regard to the established churches of these nations, believing that any so-called Christian must be tainted by their submission to Communist authorities and propaganda.

Likewise, very few Western churches understood, or could appreciate the Orthodox concept of canonical territory, meaning "we are the church of this nation or this ethnic group, and the inhabitants there are our responsibility and should not be weaned away from what should have been their birth heritage." In addition to church or parachurch groups, the churches encountered Mormons, the Unification Church (Moonies), New Age evangelists, and Hare Krishna and other forms of Eastern religions heretofore unknown, yet attractive to young people in search of meaning for their lives in this new situation.

In a 1993 study, the Center for Civil Society in Seattle determined that approximately 760 different western religious groups, churches, and parachurch organizations were at work in former communist nations of Europe. There were 200 to 350 different groups in the Commonwealth of Independent States, 120 to 200 in Romania. In the small nation of Albania, there are more than forty evangelical groups, many of whom were described by one observer as "charismatic/Pentecostal/separatist in orientation with missionaries reflecting the highly independent traits of Western independent evangelicalism." Rarely has there been any in-depth conversation or cooperation with the Albanian Orthodox Church. (The Catholic Church has its own set of mission personnel from abroad and related problems.) Protestant missionaries during the past four years have come not only from the United States, Canada, and most countries of Western Europe, but also from Mexico, Brazil, South Africa, Korea, Australia, and New Zealand.

In speaking to delegates at the 1992 Assembly of the Conference of European Churches, Patriarch Alexy II of Moscow and All Russia, then Chairman of the Presidium and Advisory Committee of CEC, indicated his disappointment and concern about such missionary endeavors in these words:

> We thought with certitude that after we received freedom, the solidarity of our Christian brothers in the West would help us to organize and restore our witness to Christ in our country, and our catechetical and missionary work in order to enlighten those educated in atheism and still ignoring Christ. And this would be in the spirit of the manifestation of the "joint witness" to Christ excluding and condemning any proselytism which was so broadly discussed in the ecumenical movement and on which several joint agreements and declarations were adopted.

> And the long-endured and desired changes for the best came. The atheist totali-

tarian system of prohibiting the free witness to Christ broke down. And what happened?

> When the territories of central and eastern Europe were opened for the public missionary endeavor and evangelism, the peoples rooted in millennial Orthodox traditions became objects of proselytism for numerous zealots calling themselves missionaries and preachers who came from outside to the new markets. We had a different idea about the joint Christian witness and the brotherly solidarity in strengthening our preaching of Christ and promoting cooperation in the ecumenical community in conditions of freedom. But we understand also that the "wild missionary endeavor" finds no support among those our brothers in the oikoumene whom we learned to regard as our brothers over the decades. Of course our people will also survive this invasion, as it survived even worse times of persecutions and attacks from the atheist propaganda. We withstood at that time, we shall withstand also now, since God was with us at that time and will be with us now.

(Both the World Council of Churches and the Conference of European Churches have made official statements opposing proselytism in the context of

Patriarch Alexy II of Moscow and All Russia

Wolf Kutnahorsky/WCC

Hare Krishna members chanting in Wenceslas Square, Prague

their commitment to ecumenical fellowship and their common witness to Jesus Christ.)

In spite of the patriarch's words about "our brothers" in the oikoumene, numerous persons and churches from mainline denominations have also entered the region for evangelistic campaigns and church planting and the sharing of their own understanding of the gospel's mandate to "go into all the world."

A group of Russian Baptist leaders in the Commonwealth of Independent States sent an open letter "to missionary organizations interested in spreading the gospel in the former Soviet Union." They began their letter by saying, "We feel we must express to you with this letter our negative feelings and often contradictary viewpoints about evangelizing in the states of the former Soviet Union." They expressed appreciation "for the truth of the Scriptures that there is 'no border for the Word of God' confirmed by your radio ministry which made it possible for every household, over several decades, to listen to the Good News that was transmitted over the airwaves. We as your grateful listeners thank you very much for this work."

But the letter went on to outline the difficulties local churches have when missionary groups "try to use the infrastructure of the already existing churches of the country, which is still unable to withstand such pressure in terms not only spiritual, but also organizational." Second, it expressed concern about the higher salaries that Western missions pay, causing "the local missions to lose interpreters, editors, preachers and missionaries" to these foreign mission agencies. Third, they caution that "it is extremely harmful to evangelize without considering the local culture, traditions and religion. In a Muslim republic, for example, it is impossible to use the same methods of proclaiming the gospel as in a traditionally Christian country." Fourth, "many missionary organizations of the West are denominational and as a result, in our land are appearing the most unbelievable churches and congregations." Fifth, "some missions organize evangelization campaigns in our countries for which they find support from indigenous churches of different denominations. It seems there is nothing wrong with this, but we in the East lack the past experience of a tolerant cooperation so these joint campaigns often create tensions and intensify the already existing disagreements between the denominations."

How well churches will hear and respond to the concerns of this open letter is yet to be seen. It is a real test for ecumenism and for the different understanding of mission and evangelism in today's world. There is no greater emotional problem between churches in eastern Europe and the Balkans with overseas churches and independent parachurch mission sending agencies than that conjured up by the issue of proselytism both perceived and experienced.

Proselytism is not just a problem for the Orthodox, however. In a recent *East-West Newsletter* of the East-West European Relations Network from England, it has been reported that evangelical groups and sects have also begun to focus on Hungary:

They have been encouraged by the new post-communist law which says that a group needs only one hundred declared adherents to be eligible to register itself as a religion, and hence to share in the sum of 2.8 million dollars that the government has set aside for the churches. So far between 50 and 60 have registered, and this number is likely to grow. No group has yet been refused registration; and the new Society of Witches is on a legal par with the Catholic and Reformed Churches. Lay people and clergy alike hope that the law will be amended to require at least a thousand adherents and thus to some extent prevent further "degradation of religion." It is an irony that the mainstream churches might be seen to depend on (arguably anti-ecumenical) legislation emanating from a secular government in order to ensure their survival in an unfamiliar pluralist environment.

Icons: Windows for Contemplation

*Dan-Ilie Ciobotea and
William H. Lazareth*

How can the divine nature of God be conveyed in human forms? Or the invisible God apprehended through human senses? Nevertheless, the church worships, confesses and glorifies God precisely because God speaks and reveals Himself to us (Hebrews 1:1-4). But the image which the Living God reveals to us is not one of eternal solitude but one of eternal communion. God is Love because God is Triune. The mystery of the Triune God is the supreme mystery of unity and communion together.

The icon, or image, of the Holy Trinity (at right) is an expression of the Orthodox Church's adoration of the Living God. Andrei Rublev, the Russian Orthodox monk who painted it (c. 1422), intended it as an affirmation of Life amid all the daily forces of death during the Tartar Domination. In the Orthodox tradition, icons are a kind of spiritual window between earth and heaven. Through the icons, the worshipping congregation contemplates the heavenly beings and establishes a spiritual link with them.

The theologians of the early church, meditating on the mystery of the incarnation of God, found even in the Old Testament texts which speak about prefigurations of the Holy Trinity. A passage in Genesis, chapter 18, deals with a mysterious visit of three angels to Abraham in the grove of

Sihastna Monastery near Neamt, in Moldavia, Romania

A small chapel and icon workshop at prison in Fornosva, near St. Petersburg

Mamre. This visit was taken to signify a manifestation of the Holy Trinity. The Orthodox liturgical commentary says: "Blessed Abraham, thou hast seen and received the One and Triune Godhead."

Through lines and colors, the icon of the Trinity conveys the glory of the Living God who revealed Himself by the oaks of Mamre. The blue symbolizes the divinity of all Three. The gold of their halos symbolizes their holiness; the royal sceptres, the Lordship of all Three. At the same time, each Person is differentiated by attitude or by relationship to the two others and by the colors assigned to each. Similarity and difference, rest and movement, youth and maturity, joy and compassion, restraint and pity, eternity and history, these all come together. There is no separation or confusion or subordination of the Persons.

The figures of the Son and the Holy Spirit are turned towards the Father, who is the Source of their life.

This image of the divine Trinity rules out all egotism—whether individual or collective—all life-destroying separation, any subordination or leveling of persons. It invites all humanity to make this world a permanent eucharist of love, a feast of life. Created in God's image (Genesis 1:26), humanity is called to live in the image of the divine life and to share its daily bread together.

In the midst of the Holy Trinity is the Word of Life made flesh, Christ crucified and raised for the life of the world. In confessing "Jesus Christ, the Life of the World," Christians affirm both the sovereignty of the Risen Lord and the universal scope of his reign.

The cup which he blesses and offers to the world signifies the life which has become "eucharist" (*eucharistia*, thanks-giving): the gift of oneself for others and in communion with others. The cup, which in the Orthodox tradition contains both the bread and the wine, is the central message of this icon for the life of the world. The lack of daily bread, for which Christ taught us to pray, brings hunger, starvation and death to a world that is now unjustly divided between the rich and the poor. Here is the meeting of ecumenics and economics. The eucharistic cup calls for a daily sharing of bread and of material and spiritual resources with the millions of hungry people in this world. Through them God, the Trinity, comes on pilgrimage to us at every moment.

Andrei Rublev's Icon of the Trinity (c. 1422)

This article is excerpted from a document prepared for the Sixth Assembly of the World Council of Churches, July-August 1983, by Dan-Ilie Ciobotea, now Metropolitan Daniel of Isai, Orthodox Church of Romania, and William H. Lazareth, the former director of Faith and Order, World Council of Churches, and a former bishop of the Evangelical Lutheran Church in America.

The Balkans

Paul Mojzes

Former Yugoslavia — The Religious Component in the Wars

The religious communities of the former Yugoslavia welcomed the major political, social, and economic changes that marked the collapse of communism and the beginning of postcommunism in the late 1980s. Like their sister churches in other parts of central and eastern Europe they were primarily focusing on the hoped-for increase in religious liberties even though the churches of Yugoslavia enjoyed a relatively greater degree of freedom than those in other communist-dominated countries. Thus they welcomed the transition with enthusiasm and most of them plunged into the public limelight with gusto.

The people looked forward to being rehabilitated and to increasing the level of their activities. Little did they anticipate that the Yugoslav federal state, which was made up of different nationalities, would in a very short time break up under the pressures of rabid ethnic nationalism. This is the story of how the religious communities, without consciously scheming, became enmeshed in the bloody wars that broke out in 1991 and for which there is still no end in sight. This article does not aim to present the entire religious life, much of which has brighter aspects than the ones presented here, but, sadly, to show how the

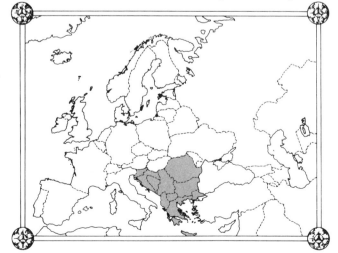

religious communities added fuel to the ethnic conflicts rather than serving as mediators or peacemakers—tasks for which they were little prepared by their past history.

The question is frequently asked whether the current wars in the Balkans are religious wars. The leaders of all major religious communities have repeatedly issued statements that the wars in Croatia and in Bosnia-Herzegovina are not religious wars. It is good that they issue such statements; if they were to say that these are wars of religions, then the followers might plunge into the battle with greater ardor.

The warfare in the former Yugoslavia, indeed, did not begin as an explicitly religious war, nor is the current character of the war primarily a religious one. These conflicts, however, do have distinct characteristics because ethnicity and religion have become so enmeshed that they cannot be separated. For this linkage, I will use the term ethno-religious. The fundamental causes of war are both ethnic and national, yet many nationalists take on a religious label as a way of expressing their identity and many religious institutions and leaders have not discouraged this process. As Bogdan Denitch, a Serb now teaching at the City University of New York, has said, "The churches are indeed both militant and national in former Yugoslav lands. The two identities thus reinforce each other."

If religions are viewed only from the perspective of their proclaimed ideals, then these wars are not religious. But religions grow beyond their original cores and inspirations. In practice, religion is often the very opposite or perversion of its authentic ideals. Religions are historically mediated, and greater or lesser discrepancies exist between their original ideals and their present-day realities.

The concrete historical forms of religions in the Balkans did contribute religious traits to the present warfare, usually in combination with ethnic and other aspects. While not every religious person or leader there is implicated in barbaric behavior, the regretful fact is that many individuals and groups have sanctioned and "sanctified" these wars.

> In practice, religion
> is often the very opposite
> or perversion of
> its authentic ideals.

The fusion or overlapping of ethnicity and religion is a well-known phenomenon in much of eastern Europe, especially in the Balkans. For centuries the church was the people and the people were the church (and a similar statement could be made about Muslims). The church envisioned its role so broadly that it contributed not only to the awakening of national consciousness but also to feelings of nationalism. The result was sometimes positive, sometimes negative. For both good and bad reasons, the communist regime in Yugoslavia tried to rupture this close identification. A generation or two grew up under Tito believing that ethnic and religious differences were not unbridgeable and that virulent ethnic nationalism had been laid to rest at the end of World War II. We now know that this was not so; the merger of ethnic and religious identification returned with such a vengeance that it is mandatory to use the single word "ethno-religious."

The large religious communities played a divisive role during the precommunist, the communist, and the postcommunist periods. Conventionally it was said that Yugoslavia was the meeting place of three great religions: Eastern Orthodoxy, Roman Catholicism, and Islam. However, Yugoslavia was in reality divided not merely into these three communities but into smaller, ethno-religious units. The Roman Catholic Church supported Croatian nationalism, the Serbian Orthodox Church supported the idea of Serbdom among the Serbs and Montenegrins, and tried even to incorporate the Macedonians. Islam contributed to the affirmations of Slavic Muslims in Bosnia-Herzegovina and adjacent areas as well as those of Albanians in Kosovo, Macedonia, and Montenegro.

Orthodox experience and history provides for the formation of national churches, whereas Catholic ecclesiology and Islamic practices avoid such an approach. However, for theological, political, and national reasons, religious leaders would frequently use the vague term "our" church when a closer examination would reveal that "our" was quite limited to their own national unit.

To put it bluntly, the leaders of each religious community justify their enthusiastic and uncritical support of rising nationalism among their peoples. Yet they condemn rival religious leaders for an "unholy" support of nationalism, which, they believe, contributed to the outbreak of the war.

Serbian Orthodox role in the disintegration

Since the Serbs had far more vested interests in keeping Yugoslavia together than the other nationalities, it may seem odd that the Serbian Orthodox Church contributed to the outbreak of hostilities, but they did so decisively. The Orthodox Church did so first by its role in the Kosovo conflict, whipping up claims of the uniqueness of Serbian victimization by others, and later by its uncritical support of Serbian nationalist aspirations.

Already in the late 1970s, the Serbian Orthodox Church was warning about the Albanian "menace" in Kosovo. The Albanian Muslim population explosion there and the exodus of Serbs was labeled as genocide of Serbs. Before too long the claim would be generalized that Serbs were threatened on all sides by conspiracies. As the Yugoslav government cracked

A Spirit of Forgiveness

Elisabeth Raiser

Dr. Elisabeth Raiser, one of the past presidents of the Ecumenical Forum of European Christian Women, writes from Novi Sad, a city in Serbia where she was the leader of a delegation of women from the Forum.

One evening, I attended the weekly ecumenical prayer service for peace, which took place in an absolutely packed synagogue in the city of Novi Sad, Vojvodina, in the former Yugoslavia. I was welcomed by the rabbi of the small but very strong Jewish community in Novi Sad. Representatives of the Jewish and Muslim communities and of the nine different Christian churches and confessions in Novi Sad (the Serbian Orthodox, Greek Catholic, Roman Catholic, Reformed, Lutheran, Methodist, and Baptist churches, and the Pentecostal and Adventist communities) spoke about mutual understanding and peace, about the victory over mistrust and hatred, about reciprocal love and mutual responsibility. Their prayers were forceful and sprang from the depth of burning hearts.

We guests from the Ecumenical Forum of European Christian Women were invited to speak, too. At the request of the interpreter, I spoke in German. Afterwards, an elderly member of the Jewish community came to me. He said, "This was the first time for forty-nine years that someone spoke German in this synagogue. The last time was when, at the order of the German occupiers, the four thousand Jews of the city were brought here before their deportation. How lovely that the language has changed so much!"

I was moved, a bit confused, and very grateful for his reconciling words. I am haunted by the idea that this man, just as all other Jews, all Muslims, all Hungarians, Slovakians, Romanians, Serbs, and Germans in this country, suffer from the blockade and embargo. What they want is peace, and they do far more for it than we in our well-heated apartments in the West. Is it not urgent for us to change our way of thinking? Should we not actively support their determination to bring about peace and democracy rather than punishing these people collectively?

—*Horizons,* July/August 1994

down on Albanian demonstrations and repeatedly repressed dissent, evoking concerns by non-Serbs about violations of Albanians' and their own rights, the Serbian Orthodox Church went on a propaganda counterattack by issuing appeals regarding alleged rapes, murders, expulsions, and the destruction of Serbian cultural monuments and sacred sites—in other words, "ethnic cleansing" of Serbs—by Albanians. One such appeal is "The Declaration of the Bishops of the Serbian Orthodox Church Against the Genocide Inflicted by the Albanians on the Indigenous Serbian Population. Together with the Sacrilege of Their Cultural Monuments in Their Own Country." This strengthened the Serb resolve not to give up Kosovo and produced a powerful anti-Albanian feeling among Serbs.

The Serbian Orthodox Church vigorously joined the Serbian Academy of Sciences and Arts in voicing Serbian grievances. The Orthodox were particularly incensed by what they regarded as the lack of

Croatian Catholic willingness to atone for their wartime crimes against the Serbian Orthodox population in Croatia and Bosnia. Prominent Serbian Orthodox bishops and theologians began speaking up on behalf of what they considered threatened Serbdom in areas where, in World War II, massacres of Serbs took place, especially the concentration camp of Jasenovac in Croatia. It was lamented that no Roman Catholic official came to the commemorations for the victims of Croatian fascist "ethnic cleansing" during the dedication of the Serbian Orthodox Church in Jasenovac in 1984. Cries of "Never again!" could be heard from both Serbian nationalist and church circles.

The Orthodox Church kept reiterating its age-old claim that it always was, is, and will be—even when all others fail—the defender of Serbian national interests. The gravest threats to Serbdom and Orthodoxy, they pointed out, were Muslims and Catholics. Two years prior to the commencement of warfare, some Serbian Orthodox publications clamored for the defense of Serbs and Orthodoxy—through military means, if necessary. The crimes of the Independent State of Croatia and the Ustashe (Croatian fascist troops in World War II) were frequently linked to the Roman Catholic Church and its leadership, and were seen as a continuation of the ages-old Catholic aspiration to convert and absorb the Orthodox into the Roman Catholic fold.

Some authors demonize the role of the Serbian Orthodox Church for allegedly always supporting the state, this in contrast to what they perceive as the much more independent role of the Catholic Church among Croatians. This author does not see any significant difference in the relationship of these two churches toward the nation they represent. It is true that the Serbian Orthodox hierarchy was more servile to the former Yugoslav government than was the Roman Catholic hierarchy, but there are a host of explanations for that. In the rise of national chauvinism, both churches have contributed heavily. The term "Serbian" seems to carry more weight than the term "Orthodox." (It remains to be seen which will win the soul of the Croats, the Catholic or the Croat identity; different Croats have made different choices, just as have the Serbs.)

Even the official documents of the Holy Assembly of Bishops use terms such as "the Christian Serbian nation" and "the Serbian Church, truly indigenous and encompassing of all the people" and thereby constantly contribute to the ethno-religious identification.

The Metropolitan of Sarajevo, Nikolaj Mrdja, was the first Serb leader to point out that organized rapes were being carried out by Serb extremists. However, at Christmas in 1992, the Orthodox hierarchy issued a sharp statement categorically denying that Serbs have organized rapes and challenging anyone to name a single concentration camp where such rapes occurred; it simultaneously charged that many Serb women had been raped by Muslims and Croats. All this indicates the delicate position of the Serbian Orthodox Church, namely to deny events that it cannot conceivably condone, and its need to be the protector of the Serbs' national reputation when the entire nation is demonized by the outside world.

When the United Nations and NATO issued an ultimatum that all the heavy weapons be withdrawn to a distance of twelve miles from Sarajevo or else they would be destroyed by air bombardment, the Holy Synod of the Serbian Orthodox Church, through its spokesman, Bishop Irinej Bulovic, issued a sharply worded statement on February 21, 1994, condemning what they considered the moral misuse of the Sarajevo shelling (which they blamed on the Muslims) for a one-sided attack upon Serbs. They warned that such an action by NATO could spread the war to other parts of the Balkans or Europe. A parallel is drawn between the threat of NATO to the Serbs and Goliath's threat to David. A peace initiative from Russia, however, was welcomed.

Neither Orthodox experience and history nor Serb nationalism is at ease with a theology of repentance and a sharp criticism of one's own nation. The same failings can be found in Catholic ecclesiology and Croat nationalism, which likewise have difficulty admitting wrongdoing by their own people. The immense transforming power of internal criticism is left unutilized by both of these Christian communities.

Individual Orthodox prelates and priests have excelled in contributing to the warfare. Some have deliberately issued false reports of destructions of Orthodox churches or murdered Serbs, knowing full well that any such claims might easily disrupt the fragile stalemate in Croatia. And finally, rather than have a calming effect, the communiqués of the entire Assembly of Orthodox Bishops tend to exacerbate the warfare by their exaggerated claims and alarmist tone, all in the name of protecting Orthodoxy and Serbdom.

Roman Catholic contribution to nationalism

In Croatia, Cardinal Kuharic's leadership has been characterized as skillfully steering the Croatian people to sovereignty. In the late 1980s, unlike his communist compatriots, the Cardinal was not timid about the defense of national sovereignty. Catholic bishops were convinced that by defending Croatian

> The immense transforming power
> of internal criticism
> is left unutilized by both of
> these Christian communities.

80

sovereignty they were doing something good. Hence, they used every opportunity to stand in defense of Croat national interests. One such opportunity was the debate about constitutional amendments concerning the name of the official language in the Socialist Republic of Croatia.

They pressed the exclusive use of the Croatian language rather than Croato-Serbian or Serbo-Croatian. Apparently the bishops and other Catholic leaders did not have the foresight that this would be threatening to the Serb population of Croatia who would interpret it as a denial of their cultural rights. (This would later be aggravated after the victory of the Croatian Democratic Union by the immediate removal of signs that were both in the Latinic script used by Croats, and the Cyrillic script used by Serbs. This could only be interpreted by the Serbs as a decision to obliterate evidence of Serb presence from Croatia. (One should note that in Serbia to this day signs and newspapers appear in both alphabets). Did not the Catholic bishops have enough wisdom to promote the rights of the Croatian people in such a way as not to threaten local minority populations? Did they not act anti-constitutionally in their advocacy of a move that would tear apart the federal structure? Surely they knew of many cases in which civil wars broke out for the preservation of a federation.

Other unconstitutional initiatives of the Catholic bishops took place. For example, as soon as they succeeded in their aim of unseating the Communist Party of Croatia and replacing it with the Croatian Democratic Union

March to United Nations on behalf of women in former Yugoslavia

Women in Black

Hedwig N. Lodwick

While living in Switzerland and being involved with Women for Peace and the Federation of Swiss Protestant Women, I joined silent candlelight vigils in Geneva on Thursday evenings in solidarity with the "Women in Black." This courageous group of women stands every Wednesday in the streets of Belgrade, capital of Serbia, protesting against the war, militarism, raping and killing, ethnic cleansing, and all forms of discrimination. Black is their color because they mourn.

"Our weekly protests," they have said, "while not massive in number, have provided a visible expression of our permanent commitment to civil disobedience and individual acts of protest. It is a symbolic witness to the horrible condition of women in the war, women who are refugees, women who care for refugees, mothers, sisters and wives of the dead, women raped in public and forced into prostitution. By our actions we denounce patriarchal and sexist origins of nationalism and of the war.

"We know that, while the men are called to die heroically for the country, the courage of women raped and killed will never be recognized except by us. We know that if we speak loud and forcefully of who we are, and what we want, our experience and our words will not enter in any political model recognized by historians of this period. Nevertheless, we are here and we will continue to be here to demonstrate our faith in the restoration of humanity."

But their voices and simple actions have been more than a silent witness. They have been recognized and heard, and have galvanized women

81

all across Europe and even North America to protest this violence. In Italy, Germany, Belgium, Great Britain, and Switzerland, women gather in solidarity with the Women in Black and this has opened for us a new consciousness of women and country, national identity and identity of the sexes, women and embargoes, and women as sexual objects of war. In Geneva, we gathered in front of one of the large downtown churches each Thursday at sundown, dressed in black for a silent candlelight vigil. Sometimes we marched across one of the bridges of Lake Geneva. Sometimes we were not silent but shouted out our contempt at the violence being committed against women and children in all of the former Yugoslavia.

With women from all over Switzerland we participated in an eight-day march from Bern, the Swiss capital, to the Palais des Nations in Geneva (European headquarters of the United Nations), and presented a strongly worded petition to the United Nations demanding that rape in time of war become a "war crime, a violation of human rights" and that women be placed on international tribunals judging war crimes. In another meeting in Geneva, women from Sarajevo, Bosnia-Herzegovina, Croatia and the Yugoslav Federation wondered aloud why women are the overwhelming majority of those engaged in peace activities and in resolving the consequences of war, yet are completely excluded from decision making? Surely this is another situation where women must have the "patient impatience" of the widow in the Gospel of Luke.

Still today, women from around the world gather and will continue to gather in solidarity with a growing number of women-led movements for peace in the former Yugoslavia.

(Hrvatska Demokratska Zajednica or HDZ), they switched attention to Bosnia-Herzegovina and supported the political activity of the HDZ among Croats there in blatant contradiction of the existing law that forbade the creation of political parties based on exclusively national or religious bases. The Catholic Church suggested that this legal provision be eliminated. Catholics were encouraged by the church to form political parties along national and religious lines. They and other nationalists prevailed.

Exclusively national-religious parties were created by all: Croats, Muslims, and Serbs. They became the three major parties of Bosnia-Herzegovina. Those who know the national and religious problems of that state realize how fragile the balance of ingredients there was and that the only nonviolent alternative was for a government that could somehow keep all three national-religious groups working together in a secular context. Many believe that the Roman Catholic bishops initiated the process of ethno-religious confrontation. The outcome of that political move was nothing short of catastrophic, and the Roman Catholic leadership bears a considerable responsibility for the ensuing tragedy. The Communists, it appears, were far more realistic about the ethno-religious threat than were the Roman Catholic and Croatian leadership.

When the first free elections in Croatia resulted in the victory of the Croatian Democratic Union, and the Roman Catholic Church was finally publicly rehabilitated after years of oppression, the Catholic Church at first displayed nearly unlimited support of the new regime's superpatriotic Croatianism. The church leadership was present at the opening of the Sabor (Parliament) sessions, politicians and clergy did not fail to use photo opportunities in order to be seen together in the media, and much was done to reinforce the notion of the unity of the church, nation, and state. The Catholic leadership erroneously regarded the HDZ as a national movement rather than a political party, which is how the HDZ wishes to be represented in order to obtain a near-monopoly over Croatia. Since 1993, however, Cardinal Kuharic has felt the need to explain that he was keeping a distance between the church and the government despite efforts on part of the HDZ to present itself as pro-Catholic.

Too little repentance

Also, the church leadership vigorously promoted the cult of Alojzije Cardinal Stepinac, a controversial figure, whom the Communists had accused of complicity in forcible conversions and in the genocide of Serbs in Croatia during World War II. Insofar as the Catholic leadership rejected the labeling of the entire Croatian people (by some Serb extremists) as genocidal, and indicated that Stepinac was badly treated by the Communists, they were, of course, right. But they showed too little willingness to express regret for the massacres against Serbs in World War II, in which a number of Catholic clergy were directly involved and for which Stepinac had been held culpable. Bishop Pihler in 1963 did issue an apology asking Serbs for forgiveness, but it appears to be the single apology by a lone Croat bishop in 1963 for the massacre of anywhere from 50,000 to 700,000 Serbs!

This is not the place to discuss the numbers of massacred, which the Croats tend to diminish and the Serbs to exaggerate. Even if it were only a thousand massacred Serbs, would it not be appropriate for the entire Bishops' Conference to issue a statement of regret? After all, there were numerous attempts of forcible conversion of Orthodox to Catholicism. Such an act is ecclesiastical and repentance would be in order.

During the tense times prior to the outbreak of the current war, Serbian bishops have often pleaded with their Roman Catholic colleagues to issue a more emphatic statement of regret and condemnation of the Croat war crimes in World War II. More often than not, however, Catholic bishops have reacted by minimizing the casualties and responding that many Croats were killed after the war by Tito's partisans.

Bertalan Tamas

Hospital in Vinkovci, Croatia; patients moved to basement

This too, of course, could have been interpreted by the Serbs as a threat that the Croats were again planning a World War II-type "ethnic cleansing."

With the onset of Croat-Muslim warfare, the tone of Catholic articles about Muslims became strident, the tendentious identification being that all Muslim combatants are *mujahedin*. The proclamation of the Croat Republic of Herzeg-Bosnia was at first welcomed by Catholic Church leaders. Later, they distanced themselves, seemingly for the sole reason of saving the Catholic presence in other parts of Bosnia. And while the Catholic bishops in Bosnia began to depart from the official policy of the Tudjman government toward prospective partitioning of Bosnia, their statements were a veritable test case of the ethno-religious formula of fusing Catholic with Croat. Little concern for the fate of non-Croat Catholics is evident, much less for non-Catholics.

Bosnian Muslims: Ethno-religious ambiguity

The Bosnian Muslims are in the unique and somewhat awkward position of being the only group of Muslims in the world who are considered Muslim both by religion and by nationality. Some claim that national consciousness among the Slavic Muslims of Bosnia-Herzegovina came late. Others maintain that the Muslims were the mainstream of Bosnian life, having come peacefully to Bosnia in the ninth century and created a Muslim civilization, culture, language, script, and so forth. However, most scholars contend that Christians of the former Bosnian Church (along with some Catholics and Orthodox), underwent a mass conversion to Islam from 1436 onward. One thing is sure: Most contemporary Slavic Muslims do not remember their pre-Islamic religious or ethnic origin. Since they were the ruling class during the rule of the Ottomans, they were detested by their neighboring Slavic Christians, Orthodox and Catholic.

When the Turks withdrew from the Balkan peninsula, it was expected that the Slavic Muslims would return to their Christian origins, thereby swelling the ranks of the Orthodox and Catholic churches. When this courting of the Muslims turned out to be unsuccessful, the surrounding Christian populations continued in their resentment and eventually began to subjugate them in order to prevent any possibility of Muslims' lording over them again. The Muslims who, heretofore, had had a fairly vague identity now had to work on a clearer one. Some preferred to call themselves Yugoslavs, some Bosnjaks, others Muslims. The Croats and the Serbs vigorously continued to claim that all the Muslims had been converts from the two respective religions and nationalities. It is in fact most likely that both Serbian Orthodox and Croatian Catholics, as well as Bogumils, a medieval Christian heresy of the Bosnian Church, converted, and, in any case, repressed their previous identities so effectively that most of them do not care to regard themselves as one or the other.

Thus Islam became more a cultural than a religious identity for most Muslims in Yugoslavia. They may well be one of the most secularized Muslim communities in the world, gravitating toward Europe rather than the Muslim East. The current president of the Bosnian government, Alija Izetbegovic, wrote a pamphlet during his time as a Communist prisoner that some describe as Islamic fundamentalist. It is alleged that he aimed to establish Bosnia as an Islamic state in which the Muslim majority would take over totally and rule with the help of traditional Islamic law. Parts of that pamphlet do have troublesome implications for non-Muslims. However, since he was elected president of Bosnia-Herzegovina, he has consistently pledged himself to a secular, multinational and multireligious state in which everyone's rights would be respected (though some observers still think that he says this is in order to please the West). Izetbegovic does believe, nevertheless, that the Muslims are the cardinal people of Bosnia-Herzegovina and if it were not for them, Bosnia-Herzegovina would long since have been divided between Serbia and Croatia.

To bypass the unfruitful discussion of what Izetbegovic meant or did not mean to say in his "Islamic Declaration"—which people tend to interpret according to their Islamic sympathies or antipathies—one can still see that Izetbegovic's Islamic convictions contributed to the outbreak of the war. Namely, he created the Party for Democratic Action, which was almost exclusively Muslim and clearly religion-identified, and he championed the homogenization of a Muslim ethno-religious identity. He is, therefore, along with the Serb and Croat nationalists, responsible for the deterioration of the political situation.

'Holy war' mentality

Since the Western world has not given any effective assistance to the Muslims—who have become the major losers in the ensuing war—Bosnian Muslims may eventually be driven into the arms of Islamic fundamentalists, who seem more eager to assist them than do others. Some observers have already noticed, in addition to the presence of a limited number of *mujahedin* from Islamic fundamentalist countries, a growing "holy war" mentality. When predominantly Muslim military units of the Bosnian army are addressed by Muslim leaders, the speeches become religious in character. As a result, if Islamic radicalization takes place, it will be less a conscious and free decision of the Bosnian Muslims and more an act of a desperate people on the verge of extermination. Under this pressure they feel themselves forced to create a totally Muslim state or face genocide.

The battles between Muslim and Croat forces from late 1992 to early 1994 are evidence that the earlier Muslim-Croat alliance was temporary, driven only by a common hatred of the Serbs. For strategic reasons the two peoples may agree to work together, but it is not a relationship based on respect and shared interests. Whether the U.S. maneuver to create a Bosnian Muslim-Croat federation, which would then enter into a confederation with Croatia itself—a plan based on political interests rather than national—will be workable is yet to be seen. It is not clear what this plan has to offer to Bosnian Serbs. If it fails to include the Serbs, then the plan will inevitably fail to stop the war.

A Bosnian Muslim religious leader has pointed out the failure of the previous communist regime to deal with nationalism because of its avoidance of recognizing the spiritual dimension of human existence. Because of the crisis of morality under communism, it was evident that people of the former Yugoslavia were not ready for the transition toward democracy in the postcommunist period. Rather, they slipped back into primitivism. The only way the people could come to grips with conflict situations was to turn to violence. Savages and criminals came to the surface after the death of Tito. Of course, this did not happen all at once, but was the result of a long neglect of the spiritual dimension. Had people been educated in a moral atmosphere, they would not have turned to killing so heinously. The worst is yet to come if these terrorists finally assume power, for they will both subjugate people and falsify history. This will only be fodder for a new round of ethno-religious warfare in a not-too-distant future.

The Protestants, making up less than one percent of the population of the former Yugoslavia, are quite marginalized. Generally, the larger churches, Reformed and Lutheran, have tended to be churches of national minorities such as Hungarians, Slovaks, and Germans. Among the larger Yugoslav nationalities the number of Protestants was quite insignificant and played only a marginal role.

In the past, Free Church Protestants such as Baptists, Pentecostals, Seventh-Day Adventists, and Methodists tended to attract members from a variety of national groups, nurturing exemplary harmonious relationships between them, and there was hope that these good relationships could survive the war. They were also outspoken in maintaining that God is not a nationalist and that religion ought to reconcile rather than divide people.

But that was too good to be true. For one, these formerly unified churches that acted wherever they had members on the territory of Yugoslavia now found themselves in separate countries and had to break up administratively along the new nation-state principles. Then, many of the Protestant leaders in Croatia became so morally outraged at what they (along with the rest of the Croatian people) perceived as Serbian aggression that they condemned this aggression and urged foreign military intervention against Serbians. They often criticized foreigners, especially Americans, for their inaction. This incensed their fellow religionists in Serbia, and formerly close colleagues now regard the Croatian Protestants no longer as peacemakers but as supporters of the war effort.

On the whole, the Protestant communities have tended to accept the official propaganda of their respective new states, and they often interpret events the way this propaganda channels them. This does not mean that they uncritically support all the policies of their governments, but it does show that even they are unable to bridge the enormous abyss that now separates Croats and Serbs, Serbs and Macedonians.

The reconciling role

Few members of the religious communities can give a sound assessment of the situation that is not merely a reflection of what they hear from their mass media. Any dissenting views rarely receive wide circulation, and even fewer are those who decide to become activists on behalf of peace. Most religious organizations and their members see themselves as being victims of forces far too great for their modest abilities. Survival in tumultuous times is the overwhelming desire; active peacemaking is not a tradition, nor do individuals have enough psychic energy left for conflict resolution. Most are too shell-shocked by the brutality of the war and the troubled times for their communities and themselves to be able to stem the confrontational mood throughout the region. Many feel that exaggerated expectations exist abroad about the influence of the churches on political and military decisions. As one theologian said in despair, "They think that all the cardinal needs to do is to whistle and say 'Stop the war' and they will immediately carry it out."

It is difficult to have hope of a better future for the devastated and brutalized people of the former Yugoslavia, including the religious segment and its institutions. Most people expect matters to become worse before they become better. In Dante's *Inferno* there is a sign over Hell: "Abandon hope all those who enter." The people in former Yugoslavia are, indeed, closer to hell than to heaven—at least as regards life here on earth. The religious communities suffer along. Perhaps some of them will learn that inspiring national chauvinism and separatism—rather than tolerance, pluralism, and concern for fellow human beings regardless of nationality and religion— is a recipe for hell.

Paul Mojzes is professor of religious studies at Rosemont College in Pennsylvania. A native of Yugoslavia, he came to the United States in 1957. He is the editor of Religion in Eastern Europe *and the president of Christians Associated for Relationships with Eastern Europe. This article is based on research developed at greater length in his book,* Yugoslavian Inferno: Ethnoreligious Warfare in the Balkans *(Continuum, 1994).*

Cardinal, Prelate Appeal for Peace

Despite the responsibility that religious leaders share for fomenting war, several remarkable statements have been made by leaders of religious communities, both individually and in meetings with others. The most significant occasions were the meetings between Patriarch Pavle of the Serbian Orthodox Church with the head of the Roman Catholic Bishops' Conference, Franjo Cardinal Kuharic. Their first meeting was in Sremski Karlovci (Serbia) in May 1991, the second in Slavonski Brod (Croatia) in August 1991, the third in spring 1992 in St. Gallen (Switzerland), and the fourth in Geneva in September 1992. The fifth was a meeting convened by the Conference of European Churches and the European Catholic Bishops' Conference in Switzerland in early 1993 at which the Reis-ul-ulema of the Islamic Community, Jakub Selimovski, also was present. The most powerful text emerged out of the 1992 Geneva meeting, and is partially reproduced here. Of great importance in this document was the distancing the prelates took from those who would wage war in the name of their religion, saying that to do so is the greatest crime against one's own religion.

Following our prayers and conversations, we appeal with one mind and voice to the faithful of our churches, to the responsible organs of the state, to military commanders and troops, to all peoples and men and women of our common geographical and spiritual area, as well as to all international forums and institutions engaged in the search for a solution or in the provision of aid to our region and in our states; and we do not only appeal but demand, on the basis of our spiritual position and moral responsibility:

1. Immediately and without condition to cease all hostilities, all bloodshed and all destruction, in particular to stop the blasphemous and insane destruction of places of prayer and holy places, Christian and Muslim alike; and that negotiations between the warring parties be initiated without delay.

2. Immediately and without condition to liberate all prisoners of war and hostages, as well as to close all prison camps and to free all those incarcerated in this evil war.

3. Immediately and without condition to cease the inhuman practice of ethnic cleansing, by whomever it is being incited or carried out.

4. To permit all refugees and deportees to return to their homes and to ensure all bishops and priests of our churches as well as Islamic spiritual leaders free access to their flock and undisturbed exercise of their office.

5. That normal communication and unrestricted circulation be reestablished, as well as the possibility of free movement and settlement for all people, whatever their religious or national affiliation, and

6. That all suffering people be assured undisturbed and equal access to humanitarian aid.

Equally with one mind and voice we condemn all crimes and distance ourselves from all criminals, irrespective of which people or army they belong to or which church or religious affiliation they claim. We especially express our horror at the perpetration of extremely immoral misdeeds, at the mistreatment of older and younger women and girls, which only monsters can perpetrate, no matter what name they give themselves.

Before God, before humanity and before our own conscience we pledge that we will use all evangelical means and the full influence of our office and responsibility in church and society to work, in our own states and peoples, decisively and openly for peace, justice and the salvation of each and every one, for the dignity and inalienable rights of every individual and every people, for humanity and tolerance, for forgiveness and love.

We ourselves call, individually and together, for repentance before the God of love, for conversation and for service to him, that we can live anew as neighbors, friends and brothers.

Peace to all!

Aspects of Orthodox Church Life in the Balkans

Evi Voulgaraki-Pissina

(translated from Greek by Elizabeth Theokritoff)

As the natural boundary of Europe on the southeast, the Balkans have always been the meeting point of West and East, Europe and Asia, North Africa and the Middle East. The Balkans have been a crossroads of people and cultures that have sometimes clashed and fought fiercely but have more usually spread and intermingled in the same geographical area, creating strong and unbreakable ties. Even from medieval times, with the exception of the western part of the Balkans, we can see a spiritual force holding together the variegated mosaic of Balkan peoples—that of Orthodoxy.

Historically, these people have often shared a common fate. The multi-ethnic East Roman Empire of Byzantium included, and for a long time united politically, Greeks, Serbs, Bulgarians, and Albanians, and in the early days, Romanians. Less harmonious were the relations between Byzantium and the Bulgarians and on occasion, between Byzantium and the Serbians. In spite of conflicts, the cultural aura of Byzantium spread throughout the Balkans. During its decline and after its fall (Constantinople fell to the Turks in 1453), all the people of the Balkans found themselves sooner or later subjugated to the Ottoman Empire. Together they experienced nearly four centuries of often brutal political, cultural, and religious repression. Liberation movements among the Balkan peoples began in the nineteenth century, at the same time as their national self-awareness started to develop.

The Serb revolts in 1804 and 1812 and the Greek revolution of 1821 were the first of a series of successful revolutionary movements that led to the establishment of nation-states, the same as we see today, although with shifting boundaries. The national awakening of the Balkan peoples provoked a series of rivalries and wars between them, continuing into this century.

This bitter experience of constant wars led to the characterization of the Balkans as the "powderkeg of Europe." This description, in the broader historical perspective, is something of an exaggeration since it represents a temporary consequence of the violent overthrow of the Turks and the search for new identities, political entities, and organization. However, the powerkeg of Europe concept was reinforced by the Balkan Wars of 1912 and 1913 and Balkan experiences in World Wars I and II as well as the wars of the 1990s.

The Cold War division during the past forty-five years had Greece belonging to the West and the other Balkan countries aligned with the East, with obvious consequences. After the col-

Romanian flag with hammer and sickle torn out

Robert C. Lodwick

lapse of communism, a new air of freedom was accompanied by disorganization, poverty, spiritual disorientation, and, in the case of portions of the former Yugoslavia, tragic armed conflict. Today, crisis is once again a hallmark of the Balkans, and questions about its future course are pressing and critical.

Amidst the chaos, and in line with a worldwide revival in religious interest, the church seems to be alive and thriving, and the population, once again, looks to it for support and strength. Aggressive atheism has lost its luster, and a secularized approach to life seems inadequate for the difficult conditions that people face today. The churches make every effort to respond to this demand, intensifying their efforts and developing their missionary, charitable, and catechetical work, striving to cover the void left by earlier restrictions under the communist regimes.

In speaking about churches in the Balkans, we are speaking principally about the Orthodox Church. The majority of inhabitants of the Balkans are Orthodox, with a large Roman Catholic population in the northwest corner of the Balkan peninsula in Croatia and Slovenia, and parts of Albania and Romania. Muslims, of course, are scattered throughout all the Balkan countries as a result of the Ottoman occupation, either because of the presence of populations of Turkish origin or on account of massive and sometimes forced conversions to Islam. They predominate in Bosnia.

Reformed and Lutheran Churches have been present in the Balkans since the Reformation days, whereas Methodists, Baptists, Congregationalists, Pentecostals, and Seventh Day Adventists came only in the nineteenth or twentieth centuries. The Jehovah's Witnesses were victims of special repressive measures during the communist period but are flourishing in many nations today. Since 1989, many small independent evangelical churches and sects, plus the Mormons and the Unification Church (the so-called Moonies), are engaged in missionary activities throughout the Balkans. To a lesser extent, several Eastern religions are also present, sometimes promoted or led by their Western followers.

European Turkey

It is important to speak briefly of European Turkey for two reasons. First, the vast majority of Christians in the Balkans lived for centuries under Ottoman domination. A study of the position of Christians in Turkey can throw light indirectly on many aspects of the problems and on the general character of the Christian churches throughout the Balkans. The fate of the Orthodox Church in the Balkans is closely bound up with the fate of their peoples and vice versa.

A second reason is that Constantinople (Istanbul) is the headquarters of the Ecumenical Patriarchate, the spiritual center for all Orthodox. The primacy of the Ecumenical throne in Constantinople is not to be likened to the primacy of the Pope in the Vatican; it has an entirely different character. The structure of the Orthodox Church is decentralized and conciliar. The Ecumenical Patriarch, however, is the "first among equals" in the East. This is a distinction of honor and not an administrative position vis-à-vis the other Patriarchates of the East (Alexandria, Jerusalem, and Antioch), and results from the significance of Constantinople as capi-

Balkan Snapshots

ALBANIA

Albania is a unique country because in 1967 it was the first country in the world to be officially proclaimed an atheist state. Because of the degree to which religion had been stamped out, there is now considerable fluidity in people's choice of religion, with Muslims converting to Christianity and nonbelievers converting to Islam and Christianity. All religions consider Albania a mission field.

It is still impossible to tell how many committed believers there are today as religious life is only now being revived and no accurate statistics are available. Most Albanians today are Muslim. Prior to the Communist period, Muslims constituted seventy percent of the population, with a Sunni majority and a Bektash minority (a Dervish order with Shiite roots originating in Turkey). New mosques are being built thoughout the country with aid from other Muslim nations. It is interesting to note that an Athonite monk and priest, Kosmas the Aetolian, who labored for the education of the population and urged people to set up schools and teach their children to read, was venerated by both the Orthodox and the Bektashi with a monastery built in his honor by the famous Ali Pasha, a Bektashi of Ioannina.

Christianity was preached in Albania in the first centuries. According to Romans 15:19, the Apostle Paul preached as far as Illyricum. Orthodox Christians make up twenty percent of the population, most of them Albanian, but with a significant number of Greeks and a smaller number of Macedonians and Serbians. Despite their ethnic differences, the Orthodox of Albania enjoy peaceful relations, and, so far, the Orthodox Church of Albania is a model of a multiethnic church community with a single church administration.

However, its relations with the state are tense, and in the summer of 1994, according to the Ecumenical Press Service, "the church issued a strong statement calling for the return, from the government to the church, of various properties and artifacts, and condemning the open campaign of misinformation mostly by the radio and television which is leveled against the Orthodox Church of Albania and especially against our Archbishop Anastasios." In part, the tension has been caused by Albanian nationalists who are reacting to a Greek national being appointed archbishop of the Albanian Orthodox Church, once again raising the fear of Greek domination.

During World War II, the Orthodox Church played an active part in the resistance. But this did nothing to stop the pressure that began in 1947 and soon led to the arrest of its four bishops and their replacement with others who were more kindly disposed to the regime. After the persecutions of 1967 by the Hoxha Communist regime, nothing

tal of the Byzantine empire.

The historical importance of the Patriarchate of Constantinople is great also because it appreciated very early in history the importance of Christianizing the Slavs. It initiated systematic missionary efforts. In the West, its missionary work extended as far as Moravia, where St. Cyril and St. Methodius were active, while in the East it extended its mission to what is now Russia, where Christianity was accepted in 988. The Orthodox missions were linked from the beginning with the use of the Slavonic language in worship and teaching. It became a written language thanks to these early missionaries.

Since recognizing the self-government (autocephaly) of the churches of Greece (1850), Serbia (1922), Romania (1925), Albania (1937) and Bulgaria (1945), the Ecumenical Patriarchate retains the spiritual oversight of the semi-autonomous Church of Crete, the Holy Mountain

Metropolitan Daniel of Moldavia and Bukovina greets the faithful and celebrates the holy liturgy at the Orthodox Cathedral in Iasi, Romania

Prefabricated church in Albania temporarily replaces much bigger one destroyed during Hoxha regime

(Mount Athos), the Orthodox diaspora in Europe, America, and Australia, and the missionary churches of Asia. Today, the Patriarchate not only refrains from any political activity but is also hindered by the Turkish government in fulfilling its religious tasks, creating the impression of a modern-day "church in captivity." A failed attempt by Turkish extremists to bomb the Ecumenical Patriarchate in late spring 1994 raised tensions between the Greek and Turkish government and resulted in letters from Konrad Raiser, general secretary of the World Council of Churches, and Jean Fischer, general secretary of the Conference of European Churches to the Ecumenical Patriarch, Bartholomeos I, expressing their solidarity with him and with the patriarchate's ministry of peace. These letters also called on the Turkish authorities to continue providing protection to the patriarchate.

From the beginning of the twentieth century, with the Balkan Wars of 1912 and 1913 and the First World War, the Christian peoples of the Balkans were reduced in numbers by constant fighting, deportations, conversions to Islam, and mass killings. For example, before 1914 there were more than 2,100,000 Greeks in Asia Minor and Constantinople. When the Greek armies were defeated in Asia Minor in 1922, 12,000 Greeks were slaughtered in Smyrna in three days. The total number of victims from this period cannot be reckoned with precision, but it is certainly more than 500,000. In 1923 under the Treaty of Lausanne,

remained of the churches and monasteries. Eyewitnesses relate how Orthodox Christians would often wall up their icons and plaster over them so that nothing showed. They alone knew that there was an icon at a particular spot in the wall.

In 1991, after several months' delay, Bishop Anastasios Yannoulatos, the Ecumenical Patriarch's delegate to Albania, was given permission to enter the country and received a temporary residence permit. Later he was appointed the Archbishop of Albania. The Orthodox Church found it impossible to elect an Albanian bishop, because not a single celibate priest remained after the atheist terror. Archbishop Anastasios, who is Greek by origin, had extensive experience in mission and soon realized that the effort to rebuild the church had to start from scratch. His first action was to call a meeting of the few elderly clergy and laity. At once they saw to the creation of a seminary and the ordination of priests. Gradually, groups such as youth and women's associations have grown up, and church life is beginning to develop.

Roman Catholics make up ten percent of the population. As a result of its ambiguous stance during the Italian occupation of Albania during World War II, the Roman Catholic Church was subjected to extreme pressures, culminating in the execution of three bishops in 1948. More than 120 priests, monks, and nuns were executed or died in prison, especially after 1967.

Although the Roman Catholic Church suffered systematic persecutions for a long time, it is now in a relatively favorable position because of the Western orientation of the government and its great economic dependence on Italy. It also enjoys advantages in organization, leadership, and financial support, which is provided liberally from abroad. According to official statistics of February 1994, more than 150 nuns from all continents were doing missionary work in Albania.

Protestant activity in Albania began in 1890 in Korça in southern Albania through the efforts of Gjerasim Qirazi, a gifted preacher who opened the first Albanian school for girls. Within two years the newly established Protestant community had grown so large that it became necessary to purchase land for their own cemetery, since the Greek Orthodox Church refused to bury Protestants. Throughout Albania, however, the Protestant church did not grow as it had in the region of Korça and, during the Hoxha Communist period, only a tiny remnant of believers remained in what could be called an underground fellowship. In 1992, however, a national union of Protestant churches was organized. Since then, Protestant missionaries from churches around the world have come to Albania, some to work with this church and others to evangelize independently throughout the country.

Church destroyed in Croatia

1,250,000 Greeks in Turkey had to move to Greece and 400,000 Turks in Greece were required to move to Turkey.

The slaughter of the Armenians, who had no chance to flee, was even more tragic. Victims of the terrible massacres of 1894-95, and particularly 1915, numbered more than a million. This genocide of Armenians and also Greeks is seen by many to be comparable only to that of the Jews under the Nazis.

Relations between the churches and ecumenism

When one examines the religious composition of the Balkans, one can see why ecumenism is not a high priority, especially given the historical, political, and ethnic tensions between the major communities of faith. The reasons are varied and include, but are not limited to, ethnic conflict, civil wars, questions related to Eastern-rite Catholicism, and proselytism.

Three students share this room at Reformed Seminary in Cluj, Romania

In the former Yugoslavia, which is discussed more fully elsewhere in this section, relations between the Orthodox, Catholic, and Muslim communities have long gone beyond the stage of polemics to violent confrontation, with more than 250,000 persons killed and many others wounded, raped, or having become displaced persons in their own land.

Combatants on each side could tell their own stories. Orthodox Serbs feel their task is the most difficult. Not only do they have to contend with compatriots of other faiths, but with the rest of the Western world as well. From their point of view, many feel that the attitude of the West, and in particular the Vatican's involvement, is aimed one-sidedly against the Serbs and, by extension, against Orthodoxy. However far this might be from the intentions of citizens or leaders of Western countries, this view is widespread among the Orthodox of the Balkans. It is no coincidence that Bulgaria, Romania, and Greece have repeatedly opposed the prospect of the United Nations authorizing bombing raids against the Serbs, while both Turkey and Albania have supported it vigorously. For better or worse, when those on any side are threatened with war or are in the midst of war, they have little room for taking friendly ecumenical initiatives towards others, be they nations, churches, or religions.

BULGARIA

The establishment of Christianity among the Bulgarians dates from the decision of Khan Boris I (852-889) to receive Christianity and baptize his subjects. Boris' choice was of tremendous political significance. The Bulgarian people acquired a cultural and spiritual center that contributed immeasurably to their internal cohesion, and they became part of the community of Christian nations, ensuring the goodwill of Byzantium. Boris's choice to use the Slavonic alphabet led to the eventual Slavicization of the Bulgarians.

Today about eighty-five percent of the population are ethnic Bulgarians and eight percent are Turks, with smaller minorities of Macedonians and Gypsies. From its inception, the Bulgarian church found itself in the tight embrace of political powers, which were to lead it on many adventures through the coming centuries. Despite the great persecution endured by Bulgarian Christians under the communists, it proved impossible to eradicate the Christian faith. Today, the Orthodox Church claims the allegiance of eighty-four percent of the population, linking religion, ethnicity, and national identity.

In 1984 and 1985 Bulgarian authorities forced the Turks to adopt Bulgarian names. Some who refused were killed by Bulgarian troops, while others fled the country. In 1989 Bulgaria's first reform government ended this policy and granted equal rights to ethnic Turks. While Muslims, mostly of Turkish descent, are only ten percent of the population, their political party has ranked third in the free postcommunist elections, and often holds the balance of power in political developments.

Roman Catholics constitute approximately five percent of the population, with Protestants making up just over one percent. At one-tenth of one percent, the Jewish community is also very small.

The government tried to divide and conquer each religion during the Communist era, so many churches are suffering from schism and are struggling among themselves. The most painful public schism is in the Orthodox Church, where one group of priests and bishops say the present patriarch was elected illegally during the Communist regime. Synods and "rump" synods have tried to sort out the issues with the Ecumenical Patriarch, ultimately siding with the current patriarch. Church buildings, including the seminary, were occupied by the dissident group and then reoccupied by loyalists, but deep tensions still exist all the way from the patriarchate to the local parish.

GREECE

In Greece today, ninety-seven percent of the population is Orthodox Christian, and Greek Orthodox Christianity is the official state religion. In the wake of its liberation from the Ottoman Turks, the Church

The question of Eastern-rite Catholics

In 1699, Transylvania was ceded to the Austrian Empire. Two years later, after pressures and inducements, a number of Orthodox bishops were united with the Vatican while retaining mass in the ancient Byzantine liturgy. Thus was created the Eastern-rite Catholic Church (sometimes referred to as Unia, with its members being called Uniates).

The question of the Eastern-rite Catholic Church has a long, torturous history, particularly in Romania, Russia, Slovakia, Belarus, and Ukraine. Since the end of communism, it has been a special impediment, sometimes with local violence, to relations between the Orthodox Church and the Roman Catholic Church. This issue has led the Orthodox to withdraw from the International Joint Committee for Theological Dialogue between Orthodox and Roman Catholics, and repeatedly to refuse invitations to participate in conferences of Roman Catholic bishops. In the document produced by the synod of heads of Orthodox churches, which met at the headquarters of the Ecumenical Patriarchate in Constantinople (Istanbul) in March 1992, the question of Eastern-rite Catholics was referred to as one of the main problems now facing the church.

The Eastern-rite Catholic Church is seen by some Christians as a successful and positive model for rapprochement between the churches in that it combined the union of a church with the Vatican with respect for the local form of worship, in this case, the Byzantine rite. The Orthodox, for their part, look upon it as the Roman Catholic Church's Trojan horse, making it easy for an Orthodox congregation to become dependent on Rome without noticing any external change in the way it worships. Both Orthodox and Catholics recognize the fact that Eastern-rite Catholic

Candle-making workshop in Berat, which supplies candles to all the churches in Albania, was started with equipment and money from Greece

93

Churches were at first Orthodox churches that were coerced into a union with Rome several centuries ago, only to be again coerced to return to the Orthodox Church. This usually occurred when the churches were under foreign domination or under communist rule. Their return to Rome has split congregations that had developed their own ethos or that, only in part, had become an integral part of the Orthodox faith. The issue of property is a key factor in many disputes and lockouts have caused some congregations that have split to meet in the public square or in the courtyard beside the church building where they once worshipped.

Contrary to what is believed, this situation has not contributed to the union of the churches but has created a third church and added another ecumenical stumbling block in Romania and parts of the Commonwealth of Independent States.

Proselytism is another element that impedes churches working together. It is a painful story and is explored in more detail on pages 72-74. What is most painful to Orthodox Christians is that very conservative groups proselytize because they believe the Orthodox Church is not a true church, does not use the scriptures, lives in the past, and worships idols, a misunderstanding of the meaning of icons in Orthodox liturgy.

Reaction to the tide of westernization

Reaction to westernization is properly a cultural and political matter, but it has immediate religious ramifications as television, Hollywood films, pornography, and Western mass media flood theaters, newsstands and the air waves. In politics, many people would like to develop alliances to gradually form the basis for partial independence from the West. Culturally, there is a deep split in Balkan society that cuts right through all social classes and political mechanisms, splitting them down the middle. There are the westernizers, and those who support the traditional ways of organization and life. Between these two extremes, of course, is a host of intermediate positions and shades of opinion.

In religious life, Western influence was strong until about the 1960s. Theological education had developed on the German model. Church art had begun to imitate the Renaissance style. In Greece, two religious organizations deeply influenced by pietism, Zoe and Sotir, did significant work in the field of internal mission. With the spiritual revival in Orthodox theology since the 1960s, however, their influence has steadily diminished. At the same time, their self-contained structure, coupled with their separatist mentality, has led the majority of Greek theologians to regard them as parachurch organizations.

The opposition between westernizers and traditionalists is also a dominant theme in Romanian society. The Romanian upper class and a large part of the intelligentsia is greatly influenced by Western, particularly French, thought.

The vast majority of people in the Balkans do not think in ecumenical terms or have contact with persons of other churches. On the other hand, many spiritual figures in the church know that ecumenism does not mean rejection of a people's identity and loss of its own religious character, but an honest and equal relationship based on respect for themselves and for others.

had a vast amount of property amassed from the people's gifts. This property has gradually been expropriated by the state, or given to it when the state took over responsibility for paying the clergy.

The number of people who take part in church life is high compared with other Western European countries, and everyone joins in the great church feasts, especially Easter. Apart from local missionary and catechetical work, the Church of Greece makes a substantial contribution to the Orthodox missionary efforts in Africa and Asia, in cooperation with the responsible patriarchates and local churches.

Roman Catholics have been present in Greece since the Crusades although they make up less than one-half of one percent of the population. Numbering about 45,000, most of them live on the Aegean and Ionian Islands, which are close to Italy, and they have always maintained close links with Italy. They are engaged in notable charitable activities.

Protestants make up one-tenth of one percent of the population, and are represented chiefly by the Greek Evangelical Church (Presbyterian) founded in 1858 and the Free Evangelical Churches of Greece founded in 1908. Pentecostals are organized into eight different communities. There are no official interchurch relations between Christian denominations in Greece except via international organizations such as the World Council of Churches.

Unlike the Protestants, the Jehovah's Witnesses have made considerable progress in their mission. Appearing first around 1900, they now outnumber Catholics and Protestants, with a membership of 60,000 in 400 congregations equally distributed between Athens and the provinces. Their refusal to do military service made them attractive to a broad spectrum of Greeks who opposed the existence of military service. In the present period of political tension, with the possibility of an expanded Balkan war, doubts about military service have largely subsided and given way to concern about the effective defense of the country. For this reason, the Jehovah's Witnesses' refusal to serve in the army is now approached critically, often leading to doubts about their patriotism.

The Jewish community in Greece numbers about five thousand.

ROMANIA

Christianity came to Romania (the Roman province of Dacia) gradually, starting from the first century. According to ancient church tradition, it was first preached by the Apostle Andrew. Until late in the Middle Ages, the language of worship was mainly Latin, which, besides being the official language of the Roman and Byzantine state, was close to the common spoken language, a Latin dialect enriched with Dacian elements. The use of Latin did not imply any ecclesiastical dependence on Rome, for the Romanian

Problems in Orthodox church-state relations

Apart from the problems connected with interchurch relations, another series of problems have their roots in state intervention in church affairs. These problems affect mainly the Orthodox churches, but not exclusively. In the former Communist states all the churches, without distinction, underwent persecution. The persecution took two forms. The direct form included dismissals, imprisonment, confiscation of property, and deprivation of human rights for those who practiced religion or taught it to their children. The indirect form, particularly successful in Bulgaria and to some extent in Romania, was the attempt by state services to "capture" the church from within. To this end, the bishops or church leaders were pressured to go along with various wishes of the government such as restricting admission to theological studies for new students or, at times, being obliged to ordain priests who were in fact government agents. The duties of a parish priest or minister were limited to the formal celebration of the liturgy.

Today, as a result, the Orthodox, Catholic, and Protestant churches do not have enough leaders who are in a position to meet the demands of the times. After the fall of the Communist regimes, it was easy to condemn many bishops and church leaders as agents of Moscow and to create a vigorous demand for a purge. But things are never that simple. On the one hand, some individuals in the church system were not there out of faith and dedication. On the other hand, the bishops and church leaders bore a tremendous responsibility for the fate of the church, and the compromises that had to be made to ensure its survival did not necessarily make them agents or hirelings. The church will cleanse itself, but this process is lengthy and painful. This situation was perhaps one of the reasons many Western Protestant groups began evangelistic work in the Balkans without being rooted or versed in the religious culture or even being willing to work with those in national churches working for reformation.

Government intervention is not a phenomenon exclusive to Eastern

Street memorial where students were killed when coal miners descended on Bucharest, Romania

Syndesmos Orthodox youth meeting at the destroyed monastery of St. Vlassos near Durres, Albania

countries. In Greece, the junta (1967-1974) virtually liquidated the church administration, removing a host of bishops and replacing them with others who supported the regime. No legal arrangement is going to stand in the way of state intervention in the Balkans if a government decides to clash with the church or weaken it. For this reason, the churches try to demonstrate their cultural and social role and convince the representatives of the state that their presence is useful. Lately, there have been more and more signs that most of the Balkan governments look to the church as a factor for social and cultural cohesion, making a positive contribution to society as a whole.

Theological and spiritual revival

In spite of all the difficulties, an important development began in the 1960s in Balkan spiritual life. Influenced largely by the theologians of the Russian diaspora, the Orthodox of the Balkans started looking for their history and identity by going back to patristic sources—the writings of the ancient fathers like Irenaeus, Augustine, or Chrysostom. They began participating with ever greater intensity in worship and in the Eucharist, and studying and trying to imitate the lives of the saints. This movement to rekindle Orthodoxy is called neo-Orthodoxy by some. The Orthodox themselves have noted that this movement provides new inspiration in ecclesiastical and spiritual matters. In reality, however, this is a return to Christianity in its primitive form, as it has been interpreted and expressed with the passage of time from the ancient church through Byzantium down to modern times.

A flood of new popularized theological publications, both academic and pastoral, is one indication of this trend. This is particularly true in Greece, where the economic position is better, and printing presses and publishing houses abound. The Romanian Orthodox Church also publishes a tremendous amount of theological journals. Many of the Balkan countries now boast of eminent theologians who are gaining a readership within and beyond the Orthodox world.

Church was ruled by metropolitans and bishops who came under Constantinople.

The presence of Roman Catholics in Romania is linked mainly with the Hungarians, who, according to historians, crossed into Transylvania in the ninth century. Initially they embraced Orthodoxy, having become Christian through contact with the indigenous population. But the kings of Hungary, in their efforts to keep the Hungarian nation together, imposed Roman Catholicism, while themselves keeping hold of political and religious power. In 1200 the conquest of Transylvania was completed. By successive papal orders from the thirteenth century, and in 1438 by order of Sigismund of Luxemburg, Orthodox worship was outlawed and severe penalties imposed on priests and any who gave them shelter, while Romanian nobles who did not agree to embrace Roman Catholicism had their property confiscated.

When Hungary was conquered by the Turks in 1541, Transylvania became an autonomous principality under Turkish suzerainty. This coincided with the great period of the Protestant Reformation. In 1604, Stephen Bocskay led a rebellion against Austrian rule and in 1606 he was recognized by the emperor as prince of Transylvania. Bocskay was a product of the Protestant Reformation (his statue is on the famous Reformation Wall in Geneva), and under his leadership, Transylvania became the main bulwark of Protestantism in eastern

Europe, and, in the words of one scholar, the only European country of that period where Roman Catholics, Calvinists, Lutherans, and Unitarians lived in mutual tolerance.

From the middle of the sixteenth century, Lutheranism prevailed among the Saxons of Transylvania, Calvinism and Catholicism among the Hungarians. Romanians remained Orthodox, but politically their position continued to be precarious. In 1699, Transylvania was ceded to the Austrian Empire. Two years later, after pressures and inducements, a number of Orthodox bishops were united with the Vatican while keeping the Byzantine rite. Thus was created the Eastern-rite Catholic Church. Owing to fierce persecutions, the Orthodox remained without bishops until 1760. But even after this time, the Orthodox were under intense pressure until 1918. After World War I, the Romanians of Transylvania were strong enough to proclaim their union with Romania. Transylvania was then seized by Romania and was formally ceded by Hungary in the 1920 Treaty of Trianon. In World War II, Hungary annexed Northern Transylvania, but returned it to Romania after the war.

Protestants, Catholics, and Orthodox each have their own version and interpretation of the history of Transylvania. With passion, many ethnic Hungarians still call for the restoration of Greater Hungary, which includes Transylvania as

The formation of the Balkan Orthodox Youth Association (BOYA), which took place in Iasi, Romania in 1993, must be mentioned here. BOYA's aim is to build up cooperation between the Orthodox youth movements and initiatives in the Balkans. Besides encouraging communication, the association provides immediate practical help in the fields of pastoral and catechetical work, theological studies, and collection and dissemination of information. It also makes available immediate and practical humanitarian aid where there is need. The importance of youth for the future of the church is fully recognized by the Ecumenical Patriarchate, and BOYA has the strong blessing of the Balkan churches for its work among young people.

In the last two decades in Greece and Cyprus, and more recently in the former Eastern bloc, parishes are beginning to come to life. In the big cities, small groups of friends form around the church. At the same time there are many activities in public places, such as universities and cultural institutions, on questions of ethics, social organization, education, and philosophy. The presence of theologians and priests often serve as catalysts in these settings. The study of Byzantine and popular music is constantly gaining ground. Many groups are presenting new works that are substantially influenced by Byzantine music, and such leading composers as Mikis Theodorakis consider it a central source of inspiration. There is a corresponding flowering of iconography.

Scene from Varatec Convent in Moldavia, Romania

The flowering of monasticism

The renewal movement in Orthodoxy has brought many young and gifted persons to the monasteries, which are developing and reorganizing themselves all over the Balkans. Today the monasteries nourish the world with ascetic and spiritual experience. In the old days, monks came from the lowest social class, both economically and educationally, but today, many or perhaps most monks have higher education. The monasteries are once again becoming centers of spiritual life, often publishing original written or artistic works of their monks. All the monasteries make a significant contribution to the development of traditional arts, both church and secular. Although most are contemplative in nature and not activist, well as parts of Croatia, Ukraine, and Slovakia. New national legislation being proposed will forbid the teaching of Hungarian as the first language for ethnic Hungarians, even in their own private schools. Hungarian signs have been torn down by nationalist Romanians, and some ethnic Hungarians have replied in kind. Ecumenical relations have not been able to bridge the ethnic and religious gulf. Ethnic Romanians who have become Baptists or Pentecostals are considered by many Orthodox as persons who have denied their nationality.

There has always been a Jewish community in Romania, although it is much smaller now than before World War II. The Gypsies are a large community, often discriminated against for their lifestyle.

Many persons in the Orthodox Church of Romania would like the state to declare the Orthodox Church the official church of the nation. There have always been close church-state ties. The Orthodox Church is heavily involved in theological education, social service, and pastoral care. While ecumenical relations have not flourished, recently the churches formed a National Council of Churches and, with the World Council of Churches, work together on projects related to street children, health, social services, and ecology.

in certain cases the monasteries actually play a large part in the community. Some carry on charitable work or contribute to the organization of theological and academic conferences or take part in missionary work abroad as mentioned earlier.

In Greece, the women's monasteries are the majority and the most flourishing. This is because most of the Greek men who want to become monks go to the Holy Mountain (Mount Athos). Priest-monks in monasteries in Greece are usually given parish responsibilities, which is to the detriment of communal life in the monastery although to the advantage of the local church.

Sihastna Monastery near Neamt in Moldavia, Romania

Of the countries under Communism, Romanian monasteries were usually respected but not able to grow as they would have under normal circumstances. While some monasteries have only a dozen or so elderly monks, today in the region of Moldavia there are monasteries that are completely full, with hundreds of monks. The Agapia monastery for women in Romania is a small city of nuns with a very high level of education. It is internationally known because important ecumenical conferences have taken place there. When a monastery celebrates its feast day, hundreds or thousands of people usually pour in for the worship and festivities.

Throughout the Balkans today, lay participation is also of great importance in all aspects of church life. The spiritual renaissance taking place is certainly a natural historical process, but it is also the fruit of great efforts on the part of clergy and laity, the hierarchy, monastics, and ordinary believers. The church seeks to unite all and hold them together in the one body of Christ.

Evi Voulgaraki-Pissina was born in Athens in 1964. She studied theology at Athens University and subsequently at Muenster and Marburg in Germany, where she specialized in mission studies and interfaith dialogue. She has served on the Executive Committee of Syndesmos (World Fellowship of Orthodox Youth) and in the Youth Working Group of the WCC Sub-Unit on Youth. She helped set up the Balkan Orthodox Youth Association, acting as general gecretary before its official establishment in 1993. She now lives in Athens, where she is working on a doctoral thesis in mission studies at the Athens Theological Faculty.

Exclusion and Embrace:
Theological Reflections in the Wake of Ethnic Cleansing

Miroslav Volf

This article is an attempt to make sense of the demonic aggression in the Balkans today. The practice of "ethnic cleansing" is an occasion to suggest that we place the problem of otherness at the center of theological reflection on social realities. As the ghettos and battlefields throughout the world testify, the future not only of the Balkans but of the whole world depends on how we deal with ethnic, religious, and gender otherness. My response to the problem of otherness is a "theology of embrace" in which the dominant categories of "oppression and liberation" are replaced by categories of "exclusion and embrace."

In the gospels, Jesus tells a puzzling story about the unclean spirit who leaves a person only to return with seven other spirits of an even more wicked character. The new state of the person is even worse than the old (see Matt. 12:45ff). I am sometimes tempted to apply this story to the situation in Eastern Europe after the 1989 revolution. The demon of totalitarian communism has just been or is being exorcised, but worse demons seem to be rushing in to fill the empty house.

This is how I introduced a paper in April 1991 on the tasks of the churches in eastern Europe following the 1989 revolution. It was at a conference of Third World theologians in Osijek, Croatia. Some six months later, the Evangelical Theological Faculty, which hosted the conference, had to flee to neighboring Slovenia; Osijek was being shelled day in and day out by Serbian forces. What during the conference had only seemed about to happen has now in fact taken place. New demons have possessed the Balkan house, preparing their vandalistic and bloody feast, first in Croatia and then in Bosnia. Signs of their presence in other parts of eastern Europe are less tangible but real, nonetheless.

The task for eastern European churches remains the same today as it was in 1991—to ward off the onrush of both the old and the new demons. What has changed is the complexity of the task.

What are some of the key theological issues facing Christians in eastern Europe, particularly in the Balkans? When the heat of the battle subsides and attention is focused neither on killing nor on surviving, two issues are at the forefront of peoples' minds. The first is evil and sin: How does one make sense of the vicious circle of hell-deep hatred and the baffling network of small and great evils that people inflict on each other? The second is reconciliation: How do we stop the killing and learn to live together after so much mutual hatred and bloodshed have shaped our common history? These issues unite in the more abstract but fundamental question of otherness—of ethnic, religious, and cultural difference. In eastern Europe this question is seldom posed in such abstract terms and often is not asked consciously at all, but it frames all the other questions with which people are grappling in their daily lives.

Much of my reflection

One of the many homes destroyed in Croatia

Bertalan Tamas

on these issues took place as I was living and teaching in Osijek during the fall of 1992. By that time, the war in Croatia was over (or at least its first phase was), but its traces were everywhere—broken windows, scarred facades, destroyed roofs, burned and desolated houses, a ruined economy and, above all, many deep wounds in the hearts of the people. Meanwhile, the war was continuing with even greater brutality in the neighbors' courtyard. As Croatians were watching the unabated Serbian aggression in Bosnia and trying to cope with the never-ending stream of refugees, they were reliving their own war inferno. There was much pride over their newly won statehood, even if it had had to be paid in blood, but there was even more trepidation about the future: When would the powerful aggressor be stopped and brought to justice? Would Croatians ever regain the lost territories and return to their villages and cities? If they did, how would they rebuild them? The feeling of helplessness and frustration, of anger and hatred was so prevalent that it dominated every discussion and action.

> How do we stop the killing and learn to live together after so much mutual hatred and bloodshed have shaped our common history?

From the beginning of the conflict, I was sharing in the destiny of my people—first from afar, from Slovenia and from my home in California, then first-hand, when I arrived in Osijek for a prolonged stay. It was then that I was forced to start making sense of what I encountered. What I present here can best be described as a "preliminary account of an exploration." This exploration would never have been undertaken and would have long since been given up had it not been for the powerful experience of the complex and conflicting social realities brought on by revolution and war. Experience goaded me to explore, so I will not shy away from appealing to it here.

The 'other'

I was crossing the Croatian border for the first time since Croatia had declared independence. State insignia and flags that were displayed prominently at the "gate to Croatia" were merely visible signs of what I could sense like an electrical charge in the air: I was leaving Hungary and entering Croatian space. I felt relief. In what used to be Yugoslavia one was almost expected to apologize for being a Croat. Now I was free to be who I ethnically am. Yet the longer I was in the country, the more hemmed in I felt. For instance, I sensed an unexpressed expectation to explain why as a Croat I still had friends in Serbia and did not talk with disgust about the backwardness of Byzantine-Orthodox culture. I am used to the colorful surrounding of multi-ethnicity. A child of a "mixed marriage," I grew up in a city that the old Habsburg Empire had made into a meeting place of many ethnic groups, and I now live in the (tension-filled) multicultural city of Los Angeles. However, the new Croatia, like some jealous goddess, wanted all my love and loyalty and wanted to possess every part of my being. I must be Croat through and through or I was not a good Croat, I could read between the lines of the large-lettered ethnic text that met my eyes wherever I looked. "'Croatia,'" I thought to myself, "will not be satisfied until it permeates everything in Croatia."

This is easy to explain. After forced assimilation under communist rule, it was predictable that the feeling of ethnic belonging would vigorously reassert itself. Moreover, the need to stand firm against a powerful and destructive enemy leaves little room for the luxury of divided loyalties. The explanations make sense, yet the unsettling question remains: Does one not discover in Croatia's face some despised Serbian features? Has the enemy not captured Croatia's soul along with Croatia's soil? Serbian aggression has enriched the already oversized vocabulary of evil with the term "ethnic cleansing": Ethnic otherness is filth that needs to be washed away from the ethnic body, pollution that threatens the ecology of ethnic space. But, not unlike many other countries, Croatia wants to be clean, too— at least clean of its enemies, the Serbs! There is, of course, a world of difference between whether one suppresses otherness by social pressure to conform or emigrate, or even by discriminatory legislation, and whether one works to eliminate it with the destructive power of guns and fire. Is not the goal the same—a monochrome world, a world without the other?

The practice of ethnic and other kinds of "cleansing" in the Balkans forces us to place otherness at the center of theological reflection. The problem, of course, is not specific to the Balkans. The processes of integration in Europe place otherness high on the agenda. So do, for instance, the disintegration of the Soviet empire and the fragility of multi-ethnic and multireligious nations such as India. The large framework for the problem is set by developments of planetary proportions. Modern means of communication and the emerging world economy have transformed our world from a set of self-contained tribes and nations into a global city. The unity of the human race is no longer an abstract notion. The closer humanity's unity, the more powerfully we experience its diversity.

The "others"—persons of another culture, another religion, another economic status, and so on—are not people we read about from distant lands; we see them daily on the screens in our living rooms, pass by them on our streets. They are our colleagues and neighbors, some of them even our spouses. The others are among us; they are part of us, yet they remain others, often pushed to the margins. How should we relate to them? Should we celebrate their difference and support it, or should we bemoan and suppress it? The issue is urgent. The ghettos and battlefields throughout the world testify indisputably to its importance. It is not too much to claim that the future of not only the Balkans but of the whole world depends on how we deal with ethnic, religious, and gender otherness.

Both 'liberation' and 'embrace'

Liberation theologians have taught us to place the themes of oppression and liberation at the center of theological reflection. They have drawn our attention to the God who is on the side of the poor and the oppressed, as well as the demands that God's people be on the same side. Nothing should make us forget these lessons, for the "preferential option for the poor" is rooted deeply in biblical traditions. Nevertheless, the categories of oppression and liberation are by themselves inadequate to address the Balkan conflict—or, indeed, the problems in the world at large today. The categories are, of course, almost tailor-made for both Croats and Serbs: Each side perceives itself as oppressed by the other, and both are engaged in what they believe to be the struggle for liberation. Unless one is prepared to say that one side is completely right and the other wrong, this is precisely where the problem lies.

Categories of oppression and liberation provide combat gear, not a pin-striped suit or a dinner dress;

Bertalan Tamas

Bishop Endre Lange of Reformed Church of Croatia, in front of his church and manse

they are good for fighting, but not for negotiating or celebrating. Even assuming that one side is right and the other wrong, what happens when the fight is over and (we hope) the right side wins? One still faces the question of how the liberated oppressed can live together with their conquered oppressors. "Liberation of the oppressors" is the answer that the "oppression-liberation" schema suggests. But, is it persuasive? Victors are known for never taking off their soldiers' suits; liberation through violence breeds new conflicts. The categories of oppression and liberation seem ill-suited to bring about the resolution of conflicts between people and groups. I suggest that the categories of "exclusion and embrace" as two models or responses to "otherness" can do a better job. They need to be placed at the center of a theological reflection on otherness, an endeavor I call a "theology of embrace."

A theology of embrace would, however, amount to a betrayal of both God and oppressed people if it were pursued in such a way as to marginalize the problems of oppression and liberation. Rather, we need to see oppression and liberation as essential dimensions of exclusion and embrace, respectively. Those who are oppressed and in the need of liberation are always "the others." Indeed, almost invariably, the oppressed do not belong to the dominant culture of the oppressors but are persons or groups of another race, gender, or religion. To embrace others in their otherness must mean to free them from oppression and give them space to be themselves. Thus, the question must never be whether one should struggle against oppression but what theological categories are most adequate to accomplish the task.

I will address the issue of otherness by looking first at the nature of Christian identity. This will provide a platform from which to talk about sin as exclusion and about salvation as embrace.

'Aliens'

In his reminiscences, *From the Kingdom of Memory*, Elie Wiesel defined the stranger as "someone who suggests the unknown, the prohibited, the beyond; he seduces, he attracts, he wounds—and leaves . . . The stranger represents what you are not, what you cannot be, simply because you are not he . . . The stranger is the other. He is not bound by your laws, by your memories; his language is not yours, nor his silence."

How should we respond to the strange world of the other? In answering this question, Christians will have to reflect on their own identity as strangers.

From the beginning of the Christian church, otherness was integral to Christian ethnic and cultural identity. Toward the end of the New Testament period, Christians came to designate themselves explicitly as "aliens and exiles" (1 Pet. 2:11). By the second century these metaphors became central to their self-understanding. They saw themselves as heirs to the Hebrew Bible people of God: Abraham was called to go from his country, his kindred, and his father's house (Gen. 12:1); his grandchildren and their children became "aliens in the land of Egypt" (Lev. 19:34). The nation of which he and Sarah were foreparents lived as exiles in the Babylonian captivity, and, even when they lived securely in their own land, Yahweh their God expected them to be different from the nations that surrounded them. However, at the root of Christian self-understanding as aliens and exiles lies not so much the story of Abraham and his posterity as the destiny of Jesus Christ, his mission, and his rejection, which brought him to the cross. "He came to what was his own, and his own people did not accept him" (John 1:11). He was a stranger to the world because the world into which he came was estranged from God, and so it is with his followers. Christians are born of the Spirit (John 3:8) and are, therefore, not "from the world" but, like Jesus Christ, "from God" (see John 15:19). The "difference" from one's own culture—from the concrete "world" one inhabits—is essential to the Christian's cultural identity.

There are two injunctions that surface persistently in the Bible. One is to have no strange gods; the other is to love strangers. The two injunctions are interrelated: One should love strangers in the name of the one triune God, who loves strangers. This triune God is the center that regulates a Christian's relationship to otherness, a doorkeeper who opens and closes the door of the self. To be a Christian does not mean to close oneself off in one's own identity and advance oneself in an exemplary way toward what one is not. It means, rather, to be centered on this God—the God of the other—and to participate in God's advance toward where God and God's reign are not yet. Without such centeredness, it would be impossible either to denounce the practice of exclusion or to demand the practice of embrace.

> What strikes one immediately in the Balkan war is the naked hate, a hate without enough decency— or, shall we say, hypocrisy?— to cover itself up.

Exclusion

What strikes one immediately in the Balkan war is the naked hate, a hate without enough decency—or, shall we say, hypocrisy?—to cover itself up. Not that hate is unique to this conflict: Most wars feed on hate, and the masters of war know how to manufacture it well. It is the proportions of the Balkan hate and its rawness right there on the fringes of what some thought to be civilized Europe that cause us to stagger. Think of the stories of soldiers making necklaces out of the fingers of little children! Never mind whether they are true or not—that they are being told and believed suffices. The hate that gives rise to such stories and wants to believe them is the driving force behind the ruthless and relentless pursuit of exclusion known as "ethnic cleansing." This is precisely what hate is: an unflinching will to exclude, a revulsion for the other.

One of the advantages of conceiving of sin as exclusion is that it names as sin what often passes as virtue, especially in religious circles. In the Palestine of Jesus' day, "sinners" were primarily social outcasts, people who practiced despised trades, those who failed to keep the Law as interpreted by the religious establishment, and gentiles and Samaritans. A pious person had to separate from them; their presence defiled, because they were defiled. Jesus' table fellowship with social outcasts, a fellowship that belonged to the central features of his ministry, turned this conception of sin on its head: The real sinner is not the outcast but the one who casts the other out. Sin is not so much a defilement but a certain form of purity: the exclusion of the other from one's heart and one's world. In the story of the prodigal son, the sinner was not only the younger brother but also the elder brother—the one who withheld an embrace and expected exclusion. Sin is a refusal to embrace others in their otherness, a desire to purge them from one's world, by ostracism or oppression, deportation or liquidation.

Exclusion of God

The exclusion of the other is an exclusion of God. This is what one can read between the lines of the story of the prodigal son. The departure of the younger brother from the father's home was an act of exclusion. He wanted his father—and maybe his brother, too—out of his world. Yet, in his life of exclusion, in the far country, he was closer to the father than was his older brother who remained at home. For, like the father, he longed for an embrace. His older brother kept the father in his world but excluded him from his heart. For the older brother an act of exclusion demanded retaliatory exclusion. For the father an act of exclusion called for an embrace. By excluding his younger brother, the older brother excluded the father who longed for an embrace. But, did not both brothers exclude the father? Are they not both sinners? Are not both equally sinners? This brings us to the problem of the universality of sin.

From a distance, things look fairly simple in the Balkan war: Croatians and especially Muslims are the victims, and Serbians are the aggressors. Has any city in Serbia been destroyed, any of its territories occupied? The macro-picture of the conflict is clear, and it does not seem likely that anything will ever change it. I approached the clear contours of this picture with a

Waiting to enter prayer hall on Sunday afternoon in Croatia

pre-reflective expectation that the victim is innocent and the oppressor guilty. This natural presumption was aided by my belonging to the victimized group. I had, of course, never doubted that Croatians share some blame for the outbreak of the war (just as I never doubted that only Croatia's renunciation of sovereignty would have prevented the conflict from breaking out in the first place), but I expected Croatians to be more humane victims.

At night in Osijek, I would hear explosions go off and know that another house or shop of a Serb who did not emigrate had been destroyed, and rarely was anyone brought to justice. Refugees, those who were victimized the most, looted trucks that brought them help; they were at war with each other. Are these simply necessary accompaniments of a war? If so, they prove my point: The more closely one looks at the picture, the more the line between the guilty and the innocent blurs, and all one sees is an intractable maze of small and large brutalities. I was tempted to exclaim: "All are evil, equally evil!" Then I heard those same words broadcast on Serbian radio. The logic was simple: If evildoers are everywhere, then the violence of the aggressor is no worse than the violence of the victim. All are aggressors, and all are victims. Placing the micro-picture of the maze of evil so close to our eyes was calculated to remove the macro-picture of aggression and suffering from our field of vision.

Christian theology has traditionally underlined the universality of sin. "All have sinned and fall short of the glory of God," said the Apostle Paul (Rom. 3:23), echoing some central Hebrew Bible passages. In the bright light of the divine glory, stains of injustice appear on all human righteousness, and blemishes of narcissism, indifference, and sometimes hate appear on all human love. In addition to freeing us "from delusions about the perfectibility of ourselves and our institutions,"[1] the doctrine of the universality of sin pricks the thin balloons of self-righteousness of aggressor and victim alike and binds them in the solidarity of sin, thus preparing the way for reconciliation. This is why the doctrine of the universality of sin should not be given up.

If all are sinners, then are all sins equal? Reinhold Niebuhr, who in our century most powerfully restated the doctrine of the universality of sin, thought so. However, he sought to balance the equality of sin with the inequality of guilt. If one affirms the equality of sin, such a balancing act becomes unavoidable. But, why assert the equality of sin in the first place? From "all are sinners" it does not follow that "all sins are equal." Aggressors' destruction of a village and refugees' looting a truck are equally sin, but they are not equal sins. The equality of sins dissolves all concrete sins in an ocean of undifferentiated sinfulness.

This is precisely what the prophets and Jesus did not do. Their judgments are not general but specific; they do not condemn anyone and everyone, just the rich and mighty who oppress the poor and crush the needy. The sin of driving out the other from her possession, from her work, from her means of livelihood—the sin of pushing him to the margins of society and beyond—weighs high on their scales. How could there be universal solidarity in this sin? The mighty are the sinners, and the weak are the sinned against. Even if all people sin, not all sin equally. To deny this would be to insult all those nameless heroes who refused to participate in power-acts of exclusion and had the courage to embrace the other, even at the risk of being ostracized or imprisoned. The uprightness of these people demands that we talk about sin concretely.

But, if we always speak of sin concretely—if we speak of it only in the plural—do we not reduce sin to sinful acts and intentions? Is this not too shallow a view of sin, and does it not lead to unhealthy and oppressive moralizing? The answer would be yes, if it were not for the all-encompassing dimension of sin and evil.

"Eruption" might be a good word to describe the conflict in the Balkans. I am thinking here less of the suddenness by which it broke out than of its insuppressible power. It does not seem that anybody is in control. Or course, the big and strategic moves that started the conflict and keep it going are made in the centers of intellectual, political, and military power, but there is far too much will for brutality among the common people. Once the conflict started, it seemed to trigger an uncontrollable chain reaction. These were decent people, helpful neighbors. They did not, strictly speaking, choose to plunder and burn, rape and torture—or secretly enjoy these acts. A dormant beast in them was awakened from its uneasy slumber—and not only in them: The motives of those who set to fight against the brutal aggressors were self-defense and justice, but the beast in others enraged the beast in them. The moral barriers holding it in check were broken, and the beast went after revenge. In resisting evil, people were trapped by it. Evil engenders evil, and, like hot ash from the mouth of a volcano, it erupts out of aggressor and victim alike.

> Evil engenders evil, and, like hot ash from the mouth of a volcano, it erupts out of aggressor and victim alike.

Embrace

What do we do against the terrible sin of exclusion that lurks at our door or has already entered our soul? How do we master it? Is there a way out of the circle of exclusion to an embrace? The tragedy of the Balkan situation is that very few people seem to be asking these questions. Vengeance is on everybody's mind. Serbs want to avenge the slaughter of their compatriots in World War II and to repay others for their injured sense of national pride during the postwar years. Croatians and Muslims want revenge for Serbian atrocities, some from the present war and

104

some from the previous one, and for their economic exploitation. The greater their success at avenging themselves, the more Serbs feel justified in their aggression. An evil deed will not be owed for long; it demands an instant repayment in kind.

The endless spinning of the spiral of vengeance has its own good reasons that are built into the very structure of our world. If our deeds and their consequences could be undone, revenge would not be necessary. The undoing, if there were will for it, would suffice. Our actions are irreversible, however. Even God cannot change them. Therefore, the urge for vengeance or for punishment seems irrepressible. The only way out of it is through an act of forgiveness.

Forgiveness the only way

Yet, forgiveness is precisely what seems impossible. Deep within the heart of every victim, hate swells up against the perpetrator. The Imprecatory Psalms of anger and rage seem to come upon their lips much more easily than the prayer of Jesus on the cross. If anything, they would rather pray, "Forgive them not, Father, for they knew what they did" (Abe Rosenthal). If the perpetrators were repentant, forgiveness would come more easily. However, repentance seems as difficult as forgiveness. It is not just that we do not like being wrong but that, almost invariably, the other side has not been completely right either. Most confessions, then, come as a mixture of repentance and aggressive defense or even lust for revenge. Both the victim and the perpetrator are imprisoned in the automatism of exclusion, unable to forgive or repent, and united in a perverse communion of mutual hate.

In the Imprecatory Psalms, the torrents of rage have been allowed to flow freely, channeled only by the robust structure of a ritual prayer. Strangely enough, it is they that point to a way out of the slavery of hate to the freedom of forgiveness. For the followers of the crucified Messiah, their main message is that hate belongs before God—not in a reflectively managed and manicured form of a confession but as a pre-reflective outburst from the depths of our being. Hidden in the dark chambers of our hearts and nourished by the system of darkness, hate grows and seeks to infect everything with its hellish will to exclusion. In light of the justice and love of God, however, hate recedes and the seed is planted for the miracle of forgiveness. Forgiveness flounders because I exclude the enemy from the community of humans and exclude

UNHCR/A. Hollmann

Victims of 'ethnic cleansing' in northern Bosnia

myself from the community of sinners. However, no one can be in the presence of God for long without overcoming this double exclusion, without transposing the enemy from a sphere of monstrous inhumanity into the sphere of common humanity and oneself from the sphere of proud innocence into the sphere of common sinfulness. When one knows that the torturer will not eternally triumph over the victim, one is freed to rediscover one's humanity and imitate God's love for oneself. When one knows that the love of God is greater than all sin, one is free to see oneself in light of the justice of God and, so, to rediscover one's own sinfulness.

Yet, even when the obstacles are removed, forgiveness cannot simply be presumed. It always comes as a surprise—at least to those who are not ignorant of the ways of men and women. Forgiveness is an outrage, not only against the logic of the exclusion system but also "against straight-line dues-paying morality," as Lewis Smedes has suggested.[2] The perpetrator deserves unforgiveness. When forgiveness happens, there is always a strange, almost irrational, otherness at its very heart, even when we are aware that, given the nature of our world, it is wiser to forgive than to withhold forgiveness. Could it be that the word of forgiveness that must be uttered in the depths of our being, if it is uttered at all, is an echo of Another's voice?

Forgiveness is the boundary between exclusion and embrace. It heals the wounds that the power-acts of exclusion have inflicted and breaks down the dividing wall of hostility. It leaves a distance, however, an empty space between people that allows them either to go their separate ways in what is called "peace" or to fall into each other's arms.

"Going one's own way"—a civilized form of exclusion—is what the majority of the people in the Balkans contemplate in their most benevolent and optimistic moments. "Too much blood was shed for us to live together," I heard almost every time I participated in conversations about what might happen after the clamor of battle dies down. Never mind geographic proximity, never mind the communication lines that connect us, our similar languages, our common history, our interdependent economies, the complex network of friendships and relations created by the years of living with each other and making love to each other! A clear line will separate "them" from "us." They will remain "they" and we will remain "we," and we will never include "them" when we speak of "us." We will each be clean of the other and identical with ourselves, and so there will be peace among us. What muddies this clean calculation is the fact that the war broke out in the name of Serbian identity with itself. By what magic does one hope to transform exclusion from a cause of war into an instrument of peace?

The only way to peace is through embrace—that is, after the parties have forgiven and repented, for without forgiveness and repentance embrace is a masquerade. An embrace always involves a double movement of aperture and closure. I open my arms to create space in myself for the other. The open arms are a sign both of discontent at being myself only and of desire to include the other. They are an invitation to the other to come in and feel at home with me, to belong to me. In an embrace I also close my arms around the other—not tightly, so as to crush her and assimilate her forcefully into myself—for that would not be an embrace but a concealed power-act of exclusion—but gently, so as to tell her that I do not want to be without her in her otherness. I want her to remain independent and true to her genuine self, to maintain her identity and, as such, to become part of me so that she can enrich me with what she has and I do not. An embrace is a "sacrament" of a catholic personality. It mediates and affirms the interiority of the other in me, my complex identity that includes the other, a unity with the other that is both maternal (substantial) and paternal (symbolic)—and still something other than either.

(Of course, the identity of a person or a social group cannot be abstracted from its history. An embrace must include both individual histories and a common history, which is often a history of pain. The mutual inclusion of histories and of common memory is therefore essential to a genuine embrace.)

Why should I embrace the other? The answer is simple: because the others are part of my own true identity. I cannot live authentically without welcoming the others—the other gender, other persons, or other cultures—into the very structure of my being, for I am created to reflect the personality of the triune God. In the presence of the divine Trinity, we need to strip down the drab gray of our own self-enclosed selves and cultures and embrace others so that their bright colors, painted on our very selves, will begin to shine.

But how do the bright colors shine when the exclusion system is dirtying us incessantly with its drab gray paint? How do we overcome our powerlessness to resist the slippage into exclusion? We need the energies of the Spirit of embrace—the Spirit who "issues from the essential inward community of the triune God, in all the richness of its relationships," who lures people into fellowship with the triune God and opens them up for one another and for the whole creation of God.[3] The Spirit of embrace creates communities of embrace—places where the power of the Exclusion System has been broken and from whence the divine energies of embrace can flow, forging rich identities that include the other.

Miroslav Volf has been a professor of systematic theology on the Evangelical-Theological Faculty of Osijek, Croatia, since 1984, and an associate professor of systematic theology at Fuller Theological Seminary in Pasadena, California, since 1991. This article was originally presented as a paper at a conference in February 1993 in Potsdam, Germany, on the theme "God's Spirit and God's People in the Social and Cultural Upheavals in Europe." It was first published in the Journal of Ecumenical Studies, *Vol. 29, No. 2, and excerpts are reprinted here by permission of the author and the publisher.*

NOTES

[1]Walter Wink, *Engaging the Powers: Discernment and Resistance in a World of Domination* (Minneapolis: Fortress Press, 1992), p. 71.
[2]Lewis B. Smedes, *Forgive and Forget: Healing the Hurts We Don't Deserve* (San Francisco: Harper & Row, 1984), p. 124.
[3]Jürgen Moltmann, *The Spirit of Life: A Universal Affirmation* (Minneapolis: Fortress Press, 1992) p. 219.

Conclusion

John Arnold

Love Laughs at Locksmiths

In Europe the tide is pulling in two different directions at once. The western half is moving towards a high tide of integration, the eastern half towards an ebb of disintegration. Yet the recent Greek presidency of the

European Union reminds us that the dividing line cannot be drawn too neatly, that East and West need each other and that the relationship, though fruitful, will not be easy. One of the prime tasks of the churches is to sustain a vision of a whole Europe, one in which the Protestant North, the Catholic South and the Orthodox East interact for the benefit of all—and this at a time when there is a strong temptation for the West to go it alone, in a dash for affluence, and for the East to fall back into chauvinistic nationalism. To do this they will have to learn to cooperate rather than compete and to eschew the fueling of ethnic animosity. There are some signs of hope.

Since the bleakest days of the Cold War, all the major Protestant, Anglican, and Orthodox churches (altogether about one hundred churches) have lived and worked together in the Conference of European Churches. At a time when, uniquely in history, all the power of an advanced technological state went into sealing off one half of Europe from the other, it was intolerable for believers that the bonds of fel-

lowship should be determined by anything other than the gospel itself. As always, love laughed at locksmiths and fellowship was maintained and strengthened. Individual Christians and the churches themselves played a notable part in the peaceful revolution of 1989-91. Of course, there were political, economic, and military forces at work also, but the essential struggle was spiritual. What was at stake was not so much a higher standard of living and freedom to travel, important as those things were, but truthfulness in public life and a spiritual view of human destiny. The gospel provided that, incarnated both in heroic individuals and also in the churches themselves, with all their faults, weaknesses, and compromises.

John Arnold, with CEC symbol in background

Now that the euphoria of 1989 is gone, we should not be surprised at evidence of infiltration and collaboration. After all, a totalitarian state is totalitarian; it tries to control everything. The astonishing thing, the miracle of the twentieth century, is that the churches survived at all, as the only public corporate bodies not controlled by Marxist-Leninist ideology. Now, weakened by long years of persecution and more recently by recrimination, they need all the help they can get, overwhelmed as they are by new and unheard-of opportunities for witness, service, and education. What they do not need is an incursion of ignorant, arrogant, and crusading sectarians who can only add to the disintegration of societies desperately in need of unity and stability.

It might have been the case that, with the ending of the Cold War and the lifting of the Iron Curtain, the need for the Conference of the European Churches would be over. In fact, at its last assembly in Prague in 1992 the churches reaffirmed their confidence in the Conference, renewed its leadership and entrusted the Conference with many tasks. It has had some success in bringing together the warring factions of the states of the former Yugoslavia, acting in this, as in many things, together with the Council of European Bishops' Conferences (CCEE).

About half of Europe's Christians are Roman Catholics. At a time when the Roman Church is having to adjust to a considerable loss of power in traditionally Catholic lands like Spain, Italy, Portugal, and even Ireland, a strong and dynamic Polish Pope is enjoying unparalleled media attention and spiritual authority. His policies and moral teachings, however, are strongly contested both inside and outside the church, especially in the West. In the East, the Roman Catholic Church is reestablishing itself under mostly conservative leadership (which was unable to participate in the Second Vatican Council) with a vigor that annoys the majority Orthodox churches and alarms minority Protestant ones.

Meanwhile European Protestantism is exhibiting considerable theological energy. The theological faculties of northern European universities are full to overflowing. And, while the Protestant churches remain as fragmented as ever, the Leuenberg Accord of 1973, which lifted the barriers to unity between the Lutheran and Reformed churches, may help them to a more concerted witness and service. The Porvoo Common Declaration between the Anglican churches in Britain and Ireland and the Scandinavian and Baltic Lutheran churches is now in the process of

ratification. Among other things, this agreement would result in full recognition of each other's ordained ministries, and would allow intercommunion. This action, which unites about 25 million Anglicans with about 25 million Lutherans in northern Europe, was hailed by the archbishop of Canterbury as the "single most important ecumenical proposal" to come before the General Synod in many years. The Church of England has already reached an accord with the churches that comprise the Evangelical Church in Germany (EKD). Ratified in 1991, the so-called Meissen agreement acknowledges that each church's ordained ministries are "given by God," but it does not recognize them as "interchangeable."

However, the largest single task in the next decade will be the relationship between Eastern Orthodoxy and Western Europe. Not only Greece, but all the historic Orthodox lands wish to benefit from the financial, social, and political advances of the West. Yet, they have not had the experience of the long march through the Renaissance, Reformation, and especially the Enlightenment, which made these advances possible. The pillars of the European Union—the rule of law, pluralist democracy, human rights, religious freedom—cannot safely be set upon eastern soil unless adequate foundations are laid. As soon as we engage in that essential task (which has not yet been attempted even in Greece) we will discover that it cannot be a simple matter of imposing western European norms on eastern European societies. The western norms will find themselves challenged and enriched by the encounter with Orthodoxy in the European movement, just as they have in the ecumenical movement. I predict a rough ride, but it will be a journey well worth embarking upon if the European movement is to be genuinely pan-European, as it must be if it is not to stagnate.

The end of the Cold War has brought hot war back to the European mainland, in the states of the former Yugoslavia and in the Caucasus mountains, for the first time since 1945. Yet, as recently as 1989, at the European Ecumenical Assembly in Basel, representatives of all the churches said: "There are no situations in our countries or on our continent in which

> The largest single task in the next decade will be the relationship between Eastern Orthodoxy and Western Europe.

Patriarch Alexy II confers with the Rev. Joan Campbell, general secretary, NCCC-USA; the Very Rev. Leonid Kishkovsky, right, and the Rev. Charles West, left, at Moscow meeting in June, 1994 (see page 64)

violence is required or justified." As in Ulster (Northern Ireland), armed conflict in the Balkans and in the Caucasus between communities divided by religion is a standing reproach to the churches and a challenge to the ministry of reconciliation. The churches of central and eastern Europe have a special task, as they engage in the building and rebuilding of nations, to moderate the divisive effects of nationalism, not to exacerbate them.

At the same time, the churches of western, and now increasingly, of northern Europe, have to respond to a new internationalism that is in critical solidarity with the European Union and the Council of Europe. Churches that acquired their present shape and structure within national and provincial boundaries at the time of the Reformation may have difficulty adjusting to the new situation. It also challenges the form Roman Catholic internationalism has taken. The institutions of Europe, though unequivocally rejecting ecclesiastical control or interference, all welcome the active participation of the churches in the building of the New Europe. They actively seek the churches' help in giving it a soul and a heart, as well as a mind and a body, as Jacques Delors, former president of the European Commission, has said.

Increasing European integration will sharpen the questions about the relationship of Europe with the rest of the world. This is true of its immediate neighbors in the Middle East and North Africa, with Asia, with Canada and the United States of America (who are linked with Europe in the Conference on Security and Cooperation in Europe), and above all with the poorer countries of Asia, Africa, and Latin America, which need improved terms of trade even more than they need aid. Here, the importance of the GATT (General Agreement on Trade and Tariffs) cannot be overstressed. The problems associated with large scale movements of people, with refugees and migrants, will increase. And the churches will increasingly have to deal with questions not only of aid and care but also of the rebirth of right-wing populist political activity in their

Second European Ecumenical Assembly Planned for 1997

"Reconciliation: Gift of God, Source of Renewed Life" will be the theme of the Second European Ecumenical Assembly to be convened in May 1997, jointly by the Conference of European Churches (CEC) and the Roman Catholic Council of European Bishops' Conferences (CCEE). The presidents of the CEC/CCEE have addressed a joint letter to their respective member churches inviting them to prepare themselves for the second assembly. The first assembly was held in 1989 in Basel, Switzerland, addressing the issues of Peace with Justice for the whole creation.

"If we are to witness convincingly to the Christian faith within the new situation in Europe," their letter stated, "we will have to start by taking the necessary steps along the way at local, national, and regional levels. We therefore call upon our members to take initiatives, which will witness to reconciliation as God's gift to us all, deepen our love for one another as children of one Father, and strengthen our common ministry of reconciliation in the world."

midst. These are sometimes linked with a resurgence of fundamentalism and confessionalism. The ecumenical fellowship faces testing times.

But the main tests, are, as always, spiritual, even if they present themselves in other guises. As the churches of central and eastern Europe rise to the challenge of the new opportunities for evangelism and service within their societies, they have to cope with the appalling results of the long years lived in totalitarian police states. The unlocking of the secret files—and of memories—has led to endless recrimination, envy, malice, and unassuaged guilt. If Christians cannot humbly confess their sins, and if their fellow Christians cannot show mercy and forgiveness, it is unlikely that anyone else will. Yet, it is precisely these things that are in shortest supply. They are also at the heart of the gospel, which the churches are charged to bring to our fellow Europeans, who need, above all, what the Russian writer Boris Pasternak called "God's Word of Life."

Meanwhile, the Christians of western Europe need to hear again the words of Jesus: "Do not judge, so that you may not be judged" (Matt. 7:1). The Christians of western Europe need to recommit themselves to the fellowship that meant so much in the age of Marxist-Leninist hegemony. Just when European Christians are no longer cut off from one another by restriction on travel, our fellowship is jeopardized by the great financial disparity between East and West. As the French say: "Il ne faut pas remplacer le rideau de fer par un redeau d'argent" ("We must not replace the Iron Curtain by a curtain of silver"). Here is an appeal to the imagination and generosity of those who are in positions to ensure that the old political obstacles are not replaced by new financial ones.

The collapse of communism as a political system, a philosophy, a guide to life, and an object of belief has led to bewilderment, confusion and the disintegration both of individuals and of whole societies. This process has been compared with the fall of the Roman Empire in the West, from which the medieval church emerged, clinging to the wreckage and seeking to orientate itself by faith in Christ, crucified and risen from the dead, and by a view of God's providential care partially derived from the scriptures of the Old Testament and partly from its own experience of the guidance of the Holy Spirit.

But the comparison also uncovers a perennial spiritual problem. Now that there is no longer a Communist Party to blame for everything, we are confronted directly with the reality, the ubiquity, and the enormity of human sinfulness. The quiet revolution, the fall of the Berlin Wall and the dismantling of the apparatus of terror and control have not ushered in an era of peace, justice, and prosperity anymore than did the French Revolution or the October Revolution in Russia in their day. Human history under God admits of no short cuts. It was precisely the foreshortening of eschatological hope that was communism's greatest error. In every age we have to hear the message "The End is not yet." We must continue to work and pray for that kingdom that is both "not of this world" and also destined to come "on earth as it is in heaven."

The Very Reverend John Arnold is dean of Durham Cathedral in England and president of the Conference of European Churches. This article appears in a slightly different form in "Finding our Way Home Together" published by the Christian Action Journal *(1994) in association with the* Christian Socialist Movement.

Churches Seek Ways to Mark 3rd Millenium

The Conference of European Churches and the Council of European Bishops' Conferences have begun conversations concerning possible actions to commemorate the third millenium, in the year 2000. Convinced that such commemorations should be organized at the universal level, they have suggested that common ecumenical initiatives be taken by the World Council of Churches, the Ecumenical Patriarch, and the Vatican. They proposed the date of Easter 2001. In the year 2001 the date of Easter will be common to churches of the western as well as the eastern tradition for the first time since 1990. It might well offer an opportunity for events witnessing to the churches' unity in the common faith of the risen Christ.

—CEC News

An African Looks at Europe in 1994

John S. Pobee

An American leader once said that the path to tomorrow goes through yesterday. We live in an age where people are so concerned with the present, often trying to survive its cruelty, that there is a temptation to forget or ignore our yesterdays. I shall, therefore, begin my reflections from my yesterday and how Europe has traveled with me to this day.

I am an African from Ghana, formerly the Gold Coast, in West Africa, which used to be known as the White Man's Grave, because many Europeans who ventured on those shores died of malaria, yellow fever, diphtheria, and dysentery. Fairly early, efforts were made to let Africans do their own thing, for which they were offered training. I refer to African personalities like Anton Wilhelm Amo (eighteenth century) who became an idol at Wittenberg University and taught in the universities of Jena, Wittenberg, and Halle; J. E. J. Capitein (1717-1747), the first African to be ordained in a Protestant church since the Reformation; and Philip Quaque (eighteenth century), the first African to be ordained in the Anglican tradition. West Africans are a proud people, exuding a self-confidence that puts Europe in its place.

I did up to my first degree in the Gold Coast, before going to Europe for further studies in the former colonial ruler of Gold Coast, the United Kingdom. My African identity by that stage was well defined, and I was ready to encounter foreign cultures with confidence and openness. Since then I have shuffled between Africa and Europe, seemingly at home everywhere.

Archbishop Desmond Tutu in England, with Westminster Dean Michael Moyne

And so, I observe Europe as a West African, an African with considerable exposure to and experience of Europe, a Christian, an Anglican with ecumenical commitment and now as an executive of the World Council of Churches' program on Ecumenical Theological Education with programmatic responsibility for Africa, Europe, and the Middle East. These are the lenses through which I observe Europe.

Our common humanity

My first experiences in Europe were a process of reeducation about Europe and our common humanity. Colonial people were socialized into perceiving Europe as a bit of a heavenly Jerusalem, and there was a mystique surrounding white people, who have often tried to portray themselves as the paragon and paradigm of culture and civilization. However, within a day of being in London, I witnessed a white man spit openly in the streets, something we in the colonies had been taught to consider a sign of lack of culture.

Within two days of arrival, I saw two white men continuing in the street a fight that had started in a pub. I heard them speak Cockney English, which was very different from the Queen's English I had learned. I had to unlearn the stereotypes of the various regions of the world and to learn that there is a common humanity behind regional and human differentiation, and that I have a sacred and honorable place in this parliament of humanity.

Today when I encounter the violence in Northern Ireland, the increasing racism and anti-Semitism in England, France, and Germany, and the horrendous violence in the former Yugoslavia, my earlier awakening to our common humanity is reinforced. However, now I see this not as just a sociological and anthropological issue, but as a religious and spiritual question. It is a religious and spiritual matter to struggle together to express and maintain our common humanity in an age and on a continent in spiritual, social, economic, and political migration.

My involvement in an area of the ecumenical movement has made me aware of the necessity for the search for common humanity to be done ecumenically: interchurch, interfaith, intercultural, and global. There is nothing substantially different between a Roman Catholic and a Protestant death in Northern Ireland, between Orthodox and Muslim deaths in Bosnia, between communist and noncommunist suffering in any part of Europe.

Thus I am persuaded that a major task before people of faith is to find ways of fostering and protecting our common humanity today. It is only in that context that non-Europeans may find their well-being in Europe. To reach such a position, certain long standing ideologies must give way, such as the ideology of Christendom, which has shaped the ethics of Europe, and the ideologies of the superiority of peoples of the temperate zones to peoples of the tropics, which have contributed to the crusader mentality. How do we cope with the legacy of history and tradition? That is the task before us. Tradition must be treated dynamically.

Fostering a sense of community

In my earlier years in Britain, I was struck by the frequency of a certain message on radio announcements: "Will Mr. X last heard of at such and such an address some fifteen years ago, please contact his dying mother at such and such an address?" As a student at a theological college I had to visit patients in hospitals. At the geriatric hospital in Cambridge I met old women who had not seen their children for years, though they also lived in Cambridge or near Cambridge. I learned that this was symptomatic of the enthronement of individualism, and the concurrent demise of community. As an African whose self-

understanding and theory of being is communitarian, I found this mind-boggling. Thirty years have passed and the situation, if it has not worsened, has not improved.

Of course, there are pockets of communitarian sense, in southern European countries especially. But I believe that this is often experienced as the aggregate of individuals rather than a community in which we find ourselves by engagement with other people.

There are all sorts of substitute families, but the prototypical community is the family, so we need to get things right there. A task for Europe is to rediscover the true and sure springs of family and community. Religious people who talk of community as *koinonia*, or *ummah*, or *ahl-al-kitab* and *ahl-al-dhimma* have a contribution to make. This contribution has to be made ecumenically, however, for any other way leads to death and violence, as demonstrated in Northern Ireland and the former Yugoslavia.

Sociologists have argued that the sense of community is a characteristic of small-scale societies. There was a time when Europe had a sense of community, but waves of national, continental, and global consciousness have eroded community consciousness. As Africa now enters the global village, it must endeavor to find ways to shore up the sense of community in these new times.

The market over humanity?

The stress on individualism is not unrelated to economic matters. Europe knows now one gospel, that of the market. In this system many go to the wall, including those who until yesterday were, if not prosperous, at least comfortable middle class citizens. The well being of many people has been sacrificed at the altar of market forces energized by profit, efficiency, and competition. For those of us from the South this is only an extension of how we have been treated since colonial times: as producers of raw materials for the metropolises of Europe.

In Chief Seattle's encounter with U.S. government officials, he said, "After several days, the dying man does not smell the stench of his own body. If you continue polluting your bed, one night you will die suffocated by your own waste." In other words, the process of degrading others sooner or later leads to

> # Europe knows now one gospel, that of the market.

self-degradation. Religious institutions have their job cut out for them: to foster the idea that the market was made for human beings and not human beings for the market. This is a call for redefined priorities and a challenge to the ideologies of such institutions as the World Bank and International Monetary Fund.

Yearning for things spiritual

Africans seem unable to live and explain life without reference to spirits and religion. The pews in Europe are empty, however, to the surprise of Africans who were brought to Christ by European missionaries. There was a time when yearning after things of the spirit was deemed the mark of a stage of primitive savagery. Today in Europe one sees a widespread yearning for spirituality, a reaction in part to the culture of materialism that was spawned by science and technology.

However, many have taken their spirituality into their own hands and are no longer entrusting it to the religious institutions. That sometimes results in crass and crude spirituality, such as the revival of black masses, ritual murders, and other expressions of religious fanaticism, which have divided families and communities.

In this situation there are many issues the religious institutions must face, two of which I mention here: First, How do the churches ensure that they are not engaged in regurgitating past formulas and experiences but are going to the future through the past, by making the eternal Word of God heard and experienced as good news for today? The need to contextualize the gospel is as urgent for Europe today as for the rest of the world. Second, in an age of social, economic, political, and cultural migration, the question of authenticity needs to be renegotiated carefully and sensitively. This is highly tested, for example, on the matter of sexuality. The way forward is not fundamentalism but a rediscovery of the fundamentals of the faith as good news of hope, and the affirmation of people to take corporate responsibility for the faith and the community of faith. Residual faith is needed, which can go through all the changing scenes of life, singing the praises of the one God, the Creator.

It is a sign of changed times that churches in the West would like to hear a critique of their situation by an African. Historically, Africa and Africans have been treated as infants who never grow, and who have been objects of discussions and theses. This change is a little sign of the developing ecumenical

Churches to Take More Active Role in European Parliament

The greater attention given by European churches today to European political institutions was demonstrated at a special ecumenical service held in Strasbourg in September 1994 in the presence of Klaus Haensch, the president (speaker) of the European Parliament, to mark the beginning of the work of the newly elected European Parliament. It is the first time that European Protestants, Roman Catholics, Orthodox, and Anglicans have held such a joint service.

Keith Jenkins, general secretary of the European Ecumenical Commission for Church and Society (EECCS), which represents church bodies from western Europe, pleaded for European politicians to be attentive to those "who have no voice or whose voice is weak—the unemployed, the excluded and ignored, the countries of central and eastern Europe, many of the people of Africa, Asia, and Latin America. Some of the things they may want to say to us may make us uncomfortable, but to be servants of all we need to listen to them as well as those with powerful voices," he said in his sermon.

The service, ending with the sounds of Beethoven's "Ode to Joy," which also serves as the European anthem, was jointly organized by EECCS and its Roman Catholic counterpart, the Commission of the Episcopates in the European Union (COMECE), and included readings and prayers in all nine official languages of the European Union.

—Ecumenical News International 9/28

sense that the lives of North and South, East and West are inextricably linked. What happens in the one may sooner or later reach the other. Neither party is inoculated against the other. We are in this one world together and we have to find ways to talk the common language, even if in different tongues. But this common language must be guided by the values of sacrificial love and truth, justice, righteousness, and freedom, reconciliation and peace.

I make no apology for being concerned for Europe. In the wisdom of the Akan ethnic group of Ghana, there is a wise saying that the old woman nurtures the child to grow teeth and the child in turn will look after the old woman when she has lost her teeth. There is a mutuality and reciprocity for our common goal. None of us is safe when a single person in the parliament of humanity is not safe.

One last word—the need for humor. The business of living is hard enough; we should not compound it with taking life too seriously. I find Europeans, especially when they get on a religious and theological high horse, too serious and denuded of humor. God's humor in taking naughty humanity seriously should be an example for us.

John Pobee

John S. Pobee is coordinator of ecumenical theological education of the World Council of Churches. A past president of the International Association for Mission Studies, he is the author of several publications.

Glossary

ascetic:
A person, usually a monk or nun, who leads a life of contemplation and rigorous self-denial for religious purposes.

autocephalous:
An Orthdox Church that receives recognition as an independent or self-governing church, usually referred to in the context of a nation.

base community:
A gathering of Christians, often outside the church and the political power structures, studying scripture to find its relevance for their situation.

canton:
A political division in the Swiss Republic. Each canton or state has considerable autonomy except in the area of foreign affairs, the army, and the postal, telephone, and telegraph systems. Each canton has its own national Protestant church; these churches belong to the Federation of Swiss Protestant Churches.

concordat:
An agreement between the Vatican and a government of a nation, usually one with a majority Catholic population, regarding the regulation of church affairs in that country.

Counter Reformation:
The sixteenth century reform movement in the Roman Catholic Church that followed the Protestant Reformation and responded to it.

diaspora:
Any scattering of people with a common origin, background, or belief. Here it refers in particular to tiny groups of Christians of one denomination or church scattered across a nation or across the continent due to immigration, asylum, or warfare.

European Union:
As an institution, the European Union traces its roots to 1951 when France, West Germany, Italy, Belgium, Luxembourg, and the Netherlands formed the European Coal and Steel Community. In 1957 these six states created the European Economic Community. In 1973 Great Britain, Ireland, and Denmark joined the EEC. Greece joined in 1981, Spain and Portugal joined in 1986, and in October 1990, with the reunification of Germany, the former East Germany came into the fold.

In 1992, the Treaty on European Union signed in Maastricht, the Netherlands, initiated a full monetary and political union whereby citizens of any country of the European Community were free to travel across the frontiers without border checks or visa. The treaty also called for establishing common foreign and security policies for Community members. The Parliament of the European Community is located in Strasbourg, France; the Court of Justice is in Luxembourg; and the European Commission, which carries out the provisions of the treaties that created the European Community, is headquartered in Brussels, Belgium.

In 1994, Poland, Hungary, and the Czech Republic expressed interest in joining the European Union, but that discussion has been postponed. However, in 1994 Sweden and Finland agreed to membership, and in early 1995 Austria is scheduled to join the European Union, pending a favorable vote in a national referendum. Norway recently voted not to join, the only Nordic country to do so.

To preserve its neutrality, Switzerland has consistently voted not to join the United Nations or the European Union, although it has close working ties with both.

genocide:
The deliberate and systematic destruction and elimination of an ethnic, racial, religious, or cultural group.

hegemony:
Leadership or dominance, especially that of one state or nation over others.

Huguenots:
The name given to French Protestants who followed John Calvin. Their persecution in the late sixteenth and seventeenth centuries led many to flee to Switzerland, the Netherlands, and the Americas. Huguenots who remained in France received their civil rights during the French Revolution.

mujahedin:
Muslim zealots who fight in or give leadership to the struggle for independence.

oikoumene:
Derived from the Greek word meaning "to inhabit the whole world." By the fourth century, the oikoumene had come to refer specifically to the "Christian world" within the Roman Empire. Later, the word "ecumenical" became a descriptive term to apply to particular church councils and their dogmatic decisions. Today, the term ecumenical is used to imply the "whole household of God," and the ecumenical movement refers to the initiatives and activities encouraged and organized to promote Christian unity.

paradigm:
A pattern or model.

patriarch:
The highest ranking bishop of an autocephalous Orthodox Church such as the Armenian, Bulgarian, Greek, Russian, or Serbian Orthodox Church.

patriarchate:
The jurisdiction or territory of a patriarch.

proselytism:
The act of trying to convert a person, especially to one's religion.

Reformation:
The sixteenth century religious movement that aimed at reforming the Roman Catholic Church, but resulted in the establishment of Protestant churches. The movement began when Martin Luther posted his ninety-five theses on the castle church in Wittenberg, Germany. Other leaders of the Reformation included Ulrich Zwingli (Switzerland), John Calvin (France, Switzerland, and much of western Europe), and John Knox (Scotland).

Reis-ul-ulema:
The head of the religious Muslim community, recognized for his role in interpreting theology and religious law.

secularism:
The belief that religion should have no place in the functions of the state. Wherever governments or segments of society have become secular, they disregard, think inappropriate, or reject practices of religious faith and worship related to state or civic life.

Waldensian:
The Waldensians are the descendants of the followers of Peter Waldo, a twelfth-century reformer. In the sixteenth century, they joined the Protestant Reformation. The heart of the community is found in northwestern Italy, but there is also a large Waldensian community in Uruguay, resulting from Italian immigration. In 1979 the Italian Waldensians and Methodists joined together to form a single church, the Waldensian-Methodist Church of Italy with an approximate membership of 40,000 persons.

Acronyms

ACTS	Action of Churches Together in Scotland
CAREE	Christians Associated for Relationships with Eastern Europe
CCBI	Council of Churches for Britain and Ireland
CEC	Conference of European Churches
CIMADE	Comité Inter-Mouvements Auprès Des Evacués
CIS	Commonwealth of Independent States
CSCE	Conference on Security and Cooperation in Europe
ECCB	Evangelical Church of Czech Brethren
EKD	Evangelische Kirche in Deutschland (Evangelical Church of Germany)
GDR	German Democratic Republic
HDZ	Hrvatska Demokratska Zajednica (Croatian Democratic Union)
IRA	Irish Republican Army
JPIC	Justice, Peace, and the Integrity of Creation
NCCC-USA	National Council of the Churches of Christ in the USA
WCC	World Council of Churches
WSCF	World Student Christian Federation